THE INNOVATION AGE

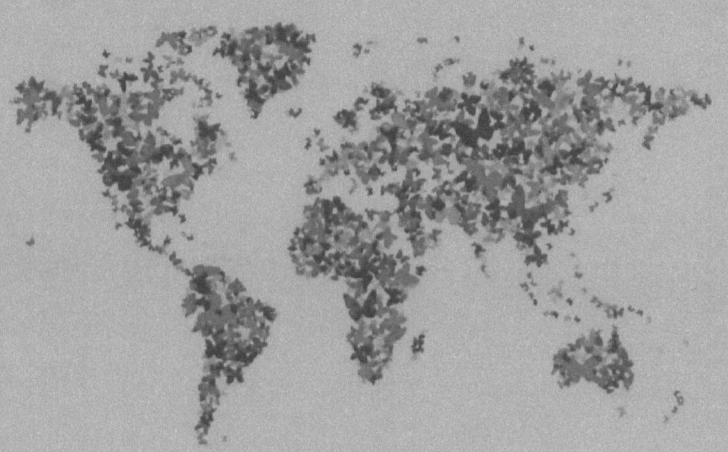

Akshay Bansal

Akshay Bansal

Dedicated to GOD

Akshay Bansal

Contents

Akshay Bansal

PREFACE

The Innovation Age: Deep connection between entrepreneurship and spirituality along with futuristic techniques of personal development and execution.

This book's main aim to make you aware about the future age of human race, with establishing a deep relation between the oldest eastern philosophy of spirituality to the western philosophy of entrepreneurship.

The flow of book is, Awareness of future age of mankind, for example transition of industrial age into information age is occurred and due to which an individual must had to change his mind set, in order to succeed, same as due to transition into innovation age from information age with all of its consequences, makes the reader aware, Also the way to cross the unproductive/ laggard to the highly productive/ innovator category which is necessary for the future age with the examples relevant for the frame work then, deep connection between spirituality and entrepreneurship is also there and also explaining how this old school will help in new age, with all the necessary information and linkage between entrepreneurship and creativity to the spirituality and how this topic is highly relevant for the next age, This book is for education and not for pleasure and will also make you aware about some most important aspects of life include both of the scenarios as of internal as well as external aspects which you encounter everyday life.

In every age there is a need of personal development, due to which in the book, there are the key points to aware the reader and take action on all the points with empowerment of the deep science of human bio and neuron chemicals, his behavior and decision making, personal strengths can be identified (which were created due to influence of upbringing) and your management style which resonate with your strengths, this book contains all and also explaining how the legends acquired the strengths in the journey of their career, for optimum productivity for example there are the techniques which will increase the human potential like 'eureka flow' in which any individual can double or triple his productivity and creativity and thieve at faster speed at work.

Critical factors are consider for the success as take a look to your past success, you will find a critical factor which is responsible for your success and this chapter is all about that factors, motivation and productivity is well consider for the career growth and due to which ,these latest techniques will make the reader more persistent and ahead of the race and of your own weak points for example techniques are design on the basis of leak points or overcome the weakness of older techniques with the realistic point of view.

This book is also related to entrepreneurship due to which business model innovation is also in the book, in which business model can be created on the basis of individual future goal, his leadership style, etc and also discussion on future technologies and with a sample business idea and model.

I hope you will like the book; as it contains great messages for your life, as well as techniques you need to try for better life, also for anything you want to communicate with me as my email is at the last page, please let me know.

Akshay Bansal

CHAPTER 1

Innovation Age: Next phase of human race

INTRODUCTION

Earth nature is always to change, as from formation of Himalayas to evolution in species for example apes evolved into humans, and when the moment came, in which apes evolved into humans, a unique characteristic also developed in them, which is lacking in all other living organism, as 'creativity' (although birds, apes and dolphins sometimes shows creativity, but, evolution and development of creative power is so slow that they can't matchup with us), a unique power to change, to think, to imagine, to execute and to create something into better, which makes us change our ages from time to time, and the more we utilize this power, learn about it and sharpen it, the shorter will be the age. We started using creativity from Stone Age, where accidental discovery makes us use of several unique things whether it is tools, fire or wheel etc, to the present age, where all of us have our own creative ideas and are not the victims of flow of human race (everyone is different due to their own unique ideas).

Evolution in ages and its environment is felt and observed by many people, from industrial age to information age (industrial age result is information age, from its elements like advancement in technology and the world war which gave rise to the computers), now, due to information age, people's life got highly influenced by connectivity, awareness and availability of vast information or we can say consequences and results of information age leads to innovation age, because of the elements like knowledge, connectivity, quick test results and feed backs, etc, which are the basic elements of creativity and innovation and due to which many innovative products like Tesla electric cars, Apple iphone etc, business models like Amazon , services like pay pal and theories like exponential theories of entrepreneurship etc. has emerged which gives rise to a viral of innovation and due to connectivity it gives power to masses to think creative and have own creative and different ideas and because of which transition will happen soon.

We are currently living in the information age, where there are plenty of information for a desired work, but, the circumstances this age is creating are not only developing the future technologies, which are AI, 3D printing etc, but also developing our creativity at utmost level (as compared to previous ages) with masses of population, due to which, employees are known as problem solver, not the industrial employee (who has to be first highly trained for certain task and employee spent whole his life in doing that single work only), following are the circumstances information age is creating which are:

1) Making the people more aware about the external (entrepreneurship, career scope etc) and internal (strengths, weakness, interests, passion etc) environment either by great connectivity and knowledge available.

2) Increasing their power of creativity (as knowledge is the tool for creativity).

3) Development and ease in business environment (financial institute, government policies and strict laws over intellectual property rights).

Above are some of the points responsible for the transitions and because of the influence it empowers most of the people physically and mentally, to promote their creative ideas and set examples for others, which ultimately spread like a viral and soon transition, will happen.

The information age will soon be move on to the innovation age, in which circumstances will be as:

1) Number of inventions will be at most.
2) Rate of change of technology will be high.
3) Business cycles of almost all the business will shrink, and only innovation can save the business.
4) Number of innovative companies will be at most.

Above are some circumstances, which innovation age will create and which will be good for innovators but might be bad for normal employees because anyone who will resist to change will suffer, Indeed this age will make much numbers of millionaires than ever and humans will be able to fight against their major enemies (which are pollution, diseases, and natural disasters, so one should be highly focused and proactive for the next age, later in this book you will be aware some of the ways to be a innovator.

Factors for transition

Pace of technology change through diverse knowledge and shared experience:

High connectivity through web and domains under the internet, not only provides social values, but also gives enormous amount of wisdom, to the mass population, due to which we don't need to start from level zero and can start from wherever we want, For example when Orkut came, it gave us great excitement of connectivity but there were still some leak points in Orkut, which were cracked and formed a new company, as Facebook and which not only made Facebook owner a billionaire, but also made him, to be a great contributor, for the transition to the next age, it's kind of reward of innovation and which shows what nature wants now from the mankind, innovation, and due to which the transition of age from information to the innovation age will be soon. Also the external environment of competition is also a forced factor, which makes us to innovate, that's why various companies are now focusing on innovation only, For example, Google which is known for its only product of search engine, is highly aware of the next age so to avoid competition, Google adopted the best strategy which is to acquire in the form of hiring highly creative people and innovative companies.

Evolution of auxiliaries for innovation age:

Evolution of innovative companies and technologies has seen from last decade, due to which, it gave the light speed to the entrepreneurs, to execute and promote their innovative ideas, for example, there are technologies like, artificial intelligence, which makes computer interaction easy, and do complex business work, Machine learning enables us, to teach the computer to perform certain complex work for us, and big data, which deals with customer data, due to which business aspects like marketing, business operations, strategy becomes so easy, that human just have to think for innovation, and machines do the rest; For example, through web forums, you noticed that, certain problem has occurred and nobody has the solution, let's say emerging entrepreneurship and an entrepreneur has a problem of finding the cofounder for his company, with whom he can share his competency, based on identification of strength and weakness, of both of entrepreneurs, along with shared vision, due to which you have created the solution of making an application (a platform for entrepreneurs to share ideas and merge together to build the company), which can be funded via innovative financial institution like VC, Angel investors, crowd funding and marketed via social media and other entrepreneurial platforms, and revenue part can be done by innovative companies like PayPal etc.

Big fish and business cycle:

Big fish eats small fish, its nature, which is also applied in business world, As small businesses are acquired by big companies, as seen in steel, automobile, telecom etc, because of the fact that, business cycles are now compacted by the impact of globalization, arbitration and high competition, which makes big fishes hungry and they have to eat the small companies, via friendly or hostile takeover, so for an individual who have big ambitions, need to go through the path of innovation (path will be discussed later), due to which this can also be the factor of transition.

Absorbing the surroundings:

Human mind works on absorption and reflection principle, the more we absorb something, the more we reflect that thing. That's why we are the average of our 5 closest friends, and in this highly capitalized world, where innovative people run the world and not the kings, humans are now surrounding with the kingdom of innovators and entrepreneurs due to which people are now absorbing innovations, ideas, which also make them a creative one, and this works at an exponential speed due to which transition is done by this factor also.

Intellectual asset vs. Physical asset:

Here idea is we have limited amount of resources on earth (which we have divided into ownership example nations) but there is another type of assets which are in limitless form which we called as intellectual assets and in future the more you have them or able to generate them via your creative mind in innovation age the more wealthier you will be, consider a small application *'snapchat'*, the creator becomes the billionaire because of this intellectual property, due to which this is also the factor of transition of information age into innovation age.

Cost and Promotion of innovative idea:

Due to innovation in financial institutions and low-cost high technology, for inventing, testing and commercializing, the ease it gives to every innovator is amazing. As in previous ages where innovators were treated as special and god gifted people, which are same as you and me just little bit more crazy about their ideas, which came from their passion and this passion came from their awareness of the purpose(power of purpose will be discussed in the next chapter) but now because of venture capitalists, angel investors, it is now not only possible to invent and commercialize, but also to become millionaire in few years(innovation age gives highest rewards to innovators), also marketing and sales which means translating value into money(the more value you create for the customer, the more money you can generate via communication or marketing) and in the information age, the cost of marketing goes down enormously, due to marketing innovation cost of marketing also going down, for example, from physical hoardings to digital marketing.

Innovators and entrepreneurs:

Innovators here not only means the inventors, who worked very hard to invent something, even many people spent their whole life to build something (which is old story, as working in collaboration make one plus one equals eleven, and gives result fast), but the people who has great ideas for anything, in any field, condition is, it should solve a problem, it can be from basic product development to business model innovation.

People need to develop themselves in their purpose, so that they can create something new, by their developed mind, which will help them sustain in the next age, because next age belongs to entrepreneurs, who always seek innovative ideas and hungry for knowledge and passionate to change the world into better, In early days, when starting a company was very difficult, and innovators were paid in the form of royalty, only if chosen by the company, but in current scenario, any inventor can start the company and eat all.

The Innovation Age

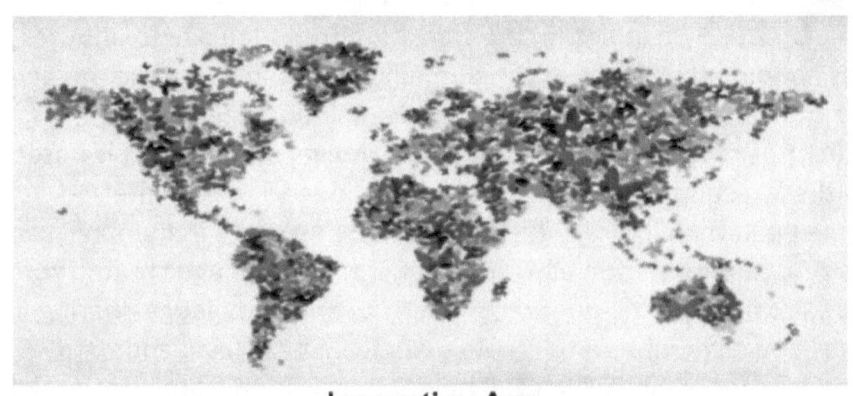

Innovation Age

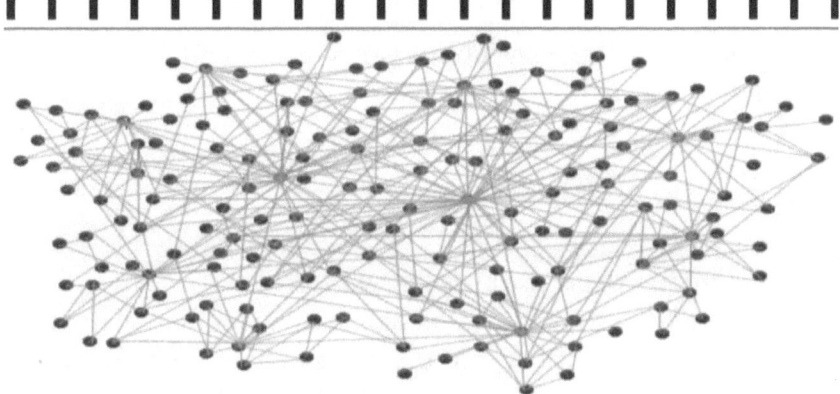

Information Age

Industrial Age

As shown in figure, the transition from one age to another, this happened because of the domain created in every age, helped the transition happened. For example, in industrial age, the industries revolution takes place and survival of the fittest is based on the latest machinery people has, and due to which, internet came up in the picture, which created the next age in human history, as information age, and even information age created some domain of creativity, due to connectivity and knowledge-sharing, it gives power to masses to create even from base level and then grow exponentially, which will help the transition from information age to innovation age.

"Innovation distinguishes between a leader and a follower"
Steve Jobs

Crossing the charm

Technique to go towards innovation
Naturally, in the innovation age, numbers of innovators or entrepreneurs, will be more, but there are people, who are not proactive or highly focused and ready for the next age, due to which, I am writing this book to reach all the people and creating awareness about the next age (which is not far away) and after awareness, anyone can be an entrepreneur/ innovator (innovator here do not means people, who invent highly scientific inventions, it can be from the basic idea of innovative comb made of wood for healthy scalp to the artificial brain of Leonardo da vinci via technology of AI, which depend from person to person).

Geoffery Moore gave a concept of *technology adoption life cycle*, in which there are innovators, early adopters, late adopters and the laggards, but he used this phenomena into marketing only. Indeed, we all fall into one of the category, which Moore mentioned and due to which, our success and life quality, depends on that particular category. Now talking about the innovators, the more will be the innovators and entrepreneurs, the more beautiful the world will be, because innovators are the people who not only create new idea but also help others accelerating their ideas. These people are always looking new things, new products for their excitement, these innovators see money, as a tool to create something new, not as the only thing to be achieved and also uses luxury, to increase their creativity and not see luxury and money as ultimate goal of life. Whereas, there are another extreme end of people, who are known as laggards, they are too lazy to change their mindset, or to become an innovator, because just like me they are born lazy, don't know their life purpose, much influenced by other people and live whole life on other's opinion, or do what other people think is cool, or maybe they think they are not capable or educated enough for invention, or similar level work, due to which they spent whole life with mediocrity, but maybe, being inventor is not possible in industrial age, and you need great education for being the one. But in information age, where availability of great knowledge, with high diversity in thinking, to make a great sense of the subject(as wisdom of people of same subject, from their own prospect, created by their creativity, which again emerges in different country say Germany and china) gives fast education to the individual, also many people think, 'it's ok being lazy', and don't do much but as innovation age will come, you won't sustain your comfortable life with this lazy mindset, because, competition is much and you need to see inside you and draw out your purpose, so that, you also can be creative and enjoying your own beautiful mind.

To cross all the categories, and reach towards the high-class category of the innovators you need a powerful tool, which is the power of purpose (as shown in figure). Also to find the purpose, the need for connectivity with the self is required, and following chapters will gives you, some of the techniques, to figure out purpose of life, because this power is the ultimate source of energy, by which we can cross not only all the competition but also all the categories, from laggards to the innovators. There are so many examples of great leaders, who once were very lazy and ordinary people, but once they got their life purpose, their speed became god speed and their contribution became our history.

Why we need to be an innovator/Entrepreneur:

1) To Enjoy our own beautiful mind
2) Contribution to the world
3) Satisfaction of life
4) Sustainability in next age

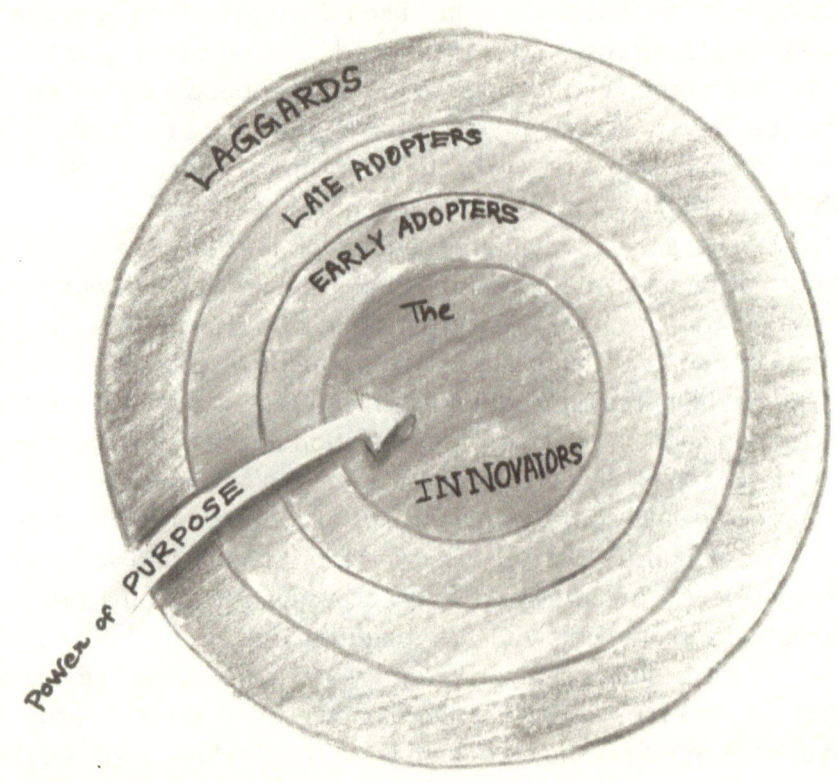

CHAPTER 2

Power of purpose for the next age

Just like a seed is responsible for a redwood, to grow faster and longer with strong roots deep into the soil, In the same way, humans need a seed of purpose, which is generated by their soul to make him/her grow, nurture and develop in the god written direction and make his roots so strong, that no competition can break him, Purpose driven life is a life, which not only fulfills the person with joy and happiness but also makes him able to contribute to the world. In your worst period, If you think life is full of sadness, and I am the most unlucky person in the world, then think again, if you don't have happiness or purpose in your life on Earth, you might burn in the hell and not came to this life, but the fact is, we all have purpose to live, reason to be happy and to make contribution to the world and spend life with joy and satisfaction, and god gives you sadness either to awake you, or to develop you or to make you realize that, your way is not the direction he choose for you, Let's take an example, Steve jobs and Elon musk, they both had extraordinary past which actually created enormous friction in their life and later this past was responsible for their development, and gave them power to think and act, due to which, they were able to connect to themselves and created a purpose for themselves and pursue it.

Consider two philosophers, one's philosophy is 'change is everything', and another is 'change is nothing', both has facts to prove their philosophy, and some people follow first one, and some follow the another, due to which, this concept gives an idea that may be possible your idea may not be comprehensible by many, but you need to have the guts to live our own life's philosophy, and then only you will be able to make your dream true and live your purpose and your own philosophy, and uses critics to modify it not to change it completely.

Belief and purpose:

The more is the vivid imagination, the more efficient ways your brain will generate to get their

To see things clear, you have to train your mind and make strong your belief in yourself, because there is a strong relation between purpose and belief, belief is the only early promoter of your purpose, for example you have created a purpose for yourself, but to act on it you need a great amount of belief, there are so many examples of people who once proved below average but after became world-renowned personalities of the world, by the power of belief (which empowered them to act) for their purpose. Because we all are wired and installed an average belief system, due to which we achieved average success, An incident, I want to elaborate here about power of purpose, I was sitting in a park after my 50 min brisk walk and doing yoga as per my morning schedule and I saw two school kids were sitting next to me, and looked like they bunked their school (as I saw other kids everyday), but this time the park caretaker scold them and make them out of the park, it made me think why they bunked the school? As education has the potential to make them out of poverty or current financial conditions, but then I realized that they don't have reason to study or purpose or anything, which will enable them to study, because belief in yourself is the first stair to success, take an example of a company Theron(an innovative blood testing company founded by Elizabeth Holmes), Holmes told in an interview that, she dropped out of the Stanford at age of 19 and started a company, and also told that, she never been on a vacation, as it might seem hard for any of us to live this kind of life, but if we go and ask her how much happy you are, she will tell that she is happy with the life, and contribution she has made, so the question is why and the answer is because, she knows her purpose which became more clear, when she saw pain of her uncle and related problems in blood industry and she decided her purpose, also if we talk about her belief, from childhood, she was motivated by her parents, that she is special and has special powers, that's is why she started so young and contributed a lot in the society and become the youngest woman billionaire in the world. We might are not as lucky as her to have parents, who believe that you are a god gifted child and will become an Einstein or Bill gates one day and install a average belief system in us(belief system is installed by wards and critical incidents by parents), due to which, we ourselves need to install a deep belief in ourselves and have to believe in yourself as much as we can, (the bigger the aim the bigger the belief required) but you need to have integrity or true to yourself, one way to increase or make stronger your belief system is via meditation.

One more story, a boy who thought himself as a complete failure and disgraced by the family also, due to which weak belief system installed in him and he was about to sell insurance door to door but by god grace he published 4 papers at the age of 25 and contribute as much as he can in his lifetime today, we remember him by his greatest theory of energy which is e=mc2 and the boy is Albert Einstein, even though weak belief system was there in the beginning, but by his inner voice made him to act on his purpose, you need to find your purpose made by your greatest strengths and insight and work on it and review your purpose in every 6 months, you can start finding your purpose by simply go to the web and fill as much questionnaire, as you can ask or to your friends or your well wishers to tell about you and by acting on the data and eventually discover the purpose, your strengths, your passion of life for which you are born.

Many people don't dare to live their purpose, because either they are insecure or they just don't know what is there in the world for them to do, then for both of the obstacles, the key solutions are:

1) **Questionnaire:** start with why for example 'why I am doing this', 'why I love books', and also ask direct self questions like 'what are my strengths or interest', and to make yourself more clear make a journal and start filling it every week with all the answers for the questions about yourself (which can be taken from web or any passion examination) and start seeing the bigger picture of your life, but not in terms of luxury but in terms of your working for example noble prize vs. Aston martin or entrepreneurship vs. luxury home remember luxury has a purpose to increase creativity, which gives enormous speed and progress to your work, (as in kingdoms kings had too much luxury because they have to grow their kingdom, and protect it so they have to be highly creative, which comes from their life style itself, as luxury promotes creativity soothe the senesces to promote the flow state).

2) **Start small:** Whatever it takes, just execute towards your dream and purpose by baby steps, and these baby steps by the time will become an athletic running, by the power of exponential growth and development. Execute, even others think it's crazy, as far as the idea makes your adenine rush too much into you, it's worth at least a try, as for my own story, I had insights for my work, but because of other's influence I was not doing that, but after one year later I found myself doing the same, imagine I had wasted my one year due to others and if you blame that in front of their faces they will say it was your choice (you need to take your life in your hands) you can't afford to say at your last day that anonymous is responsible for your failure it's you and your personal development which is responsible for your success and failure, many people spend whole life due to others, so please don't waste it and educate yourself in the area of interest passively or direct act upon it, the main point is, you need to execute somehow even if you think it might be not your ultimate life's purpose because by the time you execute you will learn great insights about yourself and even you had wrong way in the beginning, but by the midway you will definitely discover your purpose of life.

3) **Education**: If you feel insecure and don't dare to live your purpose, then develop and educate yourself, and by the time you will discover yourself and your purpose, as you will get the picture, insights about your purpose. Whole life you were living someone else life, and help them to fulfill their dream at the cost of your own, for the sake of comfort and security this is because inside you are some lazy thing, which hold you back and make a thought process which has only meant for your comfort and security, but as you read all this motivation kind of stuff you got the emotions for your life and you start thinking about it, but many times due to your own leak in will power, you might again stick to the comfort life because your body and brain takes over your soul, and as brain is also a part of body due to which, to comfort the body, brain generates the idea "you can't do it", but solution of this leakage has already taken out thousands of years ago, as to make your soul stronger than your body you need to feed it through spirituality, (which will be explained later in the book) by making your soul stronger you will be able to listen to your soul, and not to the body, and by even thinking and do small steps you will be able to achieve your dream, other than spirituality, you can also move towards your purpose via personal development, by which you will be able to learn about yourself and manage yourself and makes yourself ready to live your purpose from an upper level and no need to start small.

Purpose actually makes you a better person:

When you discover your life purpose than, rather than becoming mean, you become more socialize for the sake of your purpose, as you must know that, for a bigger purpose you need to outsource many things, and you have to go out and work with other people and socialize and also helps you to grow not only professionally but also personally, because, that passion for purpose will make your mind, to absorb good things from society, for sake of success of your aim and even not only develop you, but also to your surroundings, your purpose is not only responsible for your growth and development but also makes you highly productive, For example you have the purpose of making the platform for the people who wants to sell their highly innovative products and couldn't find any retail under consideration of innovation age, so you just have the purpose to help the innovators promote their products and to make it possible you have to develop yourself as be open-minded and ask help from others and also socialize, and by the time you work on this project, you will develop, certain more skills, in order to succeed, due to which personal development and purpose are directly proportional.

Beautiful mind and purpose of life

Movie, book and likewise industries, are based on the phenomena of imagination and creativity or we can say by a beautiful mind, where a writer or creator of an arts, who gets euphoria moments by his imaginations, make it a reality via writing or other means and let others also enjoy his beautiful mind, now imagine if everyone is so developed and creative, that he or she is able to enjoy his own imagination, which is as unique as great artists, and which can be developed by great curiosity, interest field and creativity and able to make moments a eureka moments through creativity, and feel utmost joy by that lonely moment(lonely because only one can create that imagination which is filtered by his/her knowledge, creativity ability and interest) which gives enormous pleasure of enjoying (feels like you are closer to nature, smelling flowers or listening to nature's music), this pleasure of having beautiful mind can be developed, over time by an individual with certain tools and spirituality is one of them.

Beautiful mind is like a beautiful butterfly, whose one wing is made of logic and another one is of creativity, and combined with a body of purpose which makes the butterfly fly high and spread happiness by its beauty to the world, the moment you are connected with the purpose of life, that moment and onwards you follow the path of not only career development but also your brain and thinking development within the field of purpose. For example your purpose is to merge the latest sciences and create out of the box life hacks, so you start your own YouTube channel, in which you post the videos, shows creativity around your purpose and because of your inner self-generated purpose, you thrive at much faster rate and use your beautiful mind to develop the very beautiful videos, for the people with full satisfaction of yourself and then find your work as piece of art and generated with your beautiful mind energize by the purpose.

Let us take a real life example of a beautiful mind, you go to china and experience great euphoria moments by experiencing the great architecture of the nation, that work is done because of the reason of diversity, as there is one leading company of real estate called SOHO, company's leading architect is a Baghdad's woman, who studied abroad and with huge diversity in nationality, as her class mates are of different nations with their own diverse knowledge and design, due to which she was able to design such an art cum buildings by her beautiful mind cultivated by diverse knowledge, which made many people a euphoria moment and made the owners billionaire and herself to a leading architect of the world.

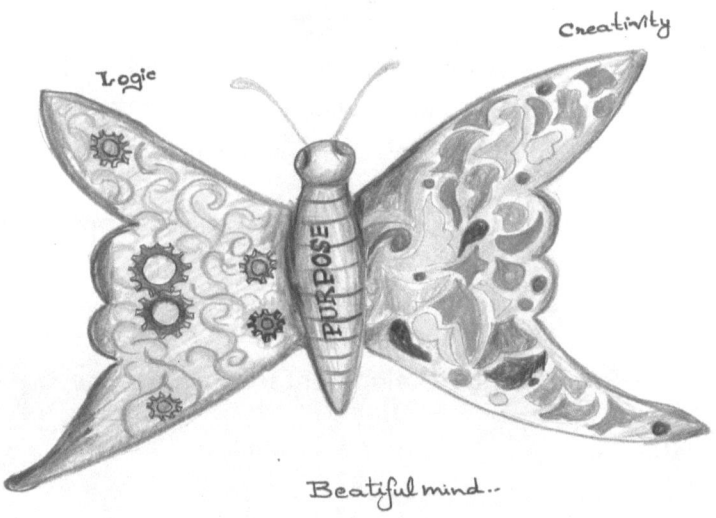

Beatiful mind...

Purpose should be to create:

To merge with the next age and to have the competitive advantage, you need to add a variable to your purpose in order to be a winner in the next age, in future the advancement of technology will eat many of the people's job as machines will be able to do all the professional work, except the most important task which only humans can do by their god gifted ability, to create and to think and due to which we will be forced to think out of the box, in order to sustain and from now on you need to be proactive in this regard, as this is survival point of view, but by adding creation and purpose makes a great combination in various regards too, which will help you to grow faster, acquire more knowledge. As **If we add the information age tools to the purpose of one's life, then it gives enormous energy to the purpose-driven being to not only life his own purpose, but also to create something or to discover something for the world and for his soul peace too.** In this highly diverse world where cognition is somehow different from each other, you need to aim at creating different there are few benefits for this

1)   You will absorb more data than before and motivated to study, as much as you can even out of the nation literature in your field of interest or purpose which makes you highly creative.

2)   A differentiation is the key strategy, adopting by various companies and due to which it gives a competitive edge to it, same as for an individual, whose purpose is merged with the creation serves him well.

3)   Growth and development for the next age.

CHAPTER 3

Spirituality and Entrepreneurship Spirituality

Inclination towards god/the ultimate cosmic energy, we live in a society where some aspects of human life are dominant, and some are submissive (logical vs. intuitional part) due to which, we all encounter almost same level of situations which creates happy and sad moments, for example we grow up, go to school then college and then job or business, and then marriage, and life goes on with same pattern, creating many moments of both the emotions of happy and sad. But God gave one aspect of life to every human, which makes him in any position of peace, joy and unique happiness, (which is above all happiness) and can't be achieved by normal pattern, but by adding a simple practice of spirituality or developing the spirituality muscles in yourself (which will move you towards enlightenment) any human can feel the difference and experience the ultimate joy of life. As people who have developed spirituality within them, are able to see the world with different angles, and which gives joyful projections unlike logical mind, which gives critical and judgmental projections of the world (which makes you defendable and in no peace situation), to test your spiritual muscles within you, simply read any spiritual article and the comprehension shows the rest.

OSHO said *'there is no other greater ecstasy than to know who you are'*, but I think, practice of spirituality is also gives the feeling of ecstasy, when we take drugs we often secrete neuron chemicals which give the flow state or the eureka moment or the feeling of ecstasy but same ecstasy can be generated by practice of spirituality.

Through spirituality various aspects of human today's life are linked, and even this eastern philosophy are now using by many nations as, productive exercise for their work and profession, because spirituality makes a person highly creative, is directly associated with creativity and human potential.

When someone consume alcohol or drug, he or she gets into the state of liberation, in which free flow of ideas gets in the mind and feeling is enormously high at a cost of reducing your conscious level, on the other hand, path of spirituality gives you a state of liberation and increases your conscious level, As swami Vivekananda once told his brother, he will die in 6 years, his brother did not like the statement, and then swami ji explain that my conscious level has increased so much, that this human body won't be able to contain me anymore, this state is called liberation, salvation, 'Buddha' position, where soul is so powerful that it does not need the human body any more.

Scientifically speaking the noticeable benefits of spirituality are:

1)   It increases our brain's gray matter (which helps in creative activity)

2)   It corrects our biochemicals and neuron-chemicals which makes us highly productive and develop the scope of increased potential.

3)   Make us more ethical and generate a great belief in our self which ultimately kills anxiety and other anti-productive cognitions of us.

4)   Developed spiritual muscles give a feeling of ecstasy without any harm

Spirituality may be mere a hypothetical phenomena for many, but once you start the journey and feel the potential you will understand its credibility for life, For example, after study of the molecular chemistry, you develop a mindset which helps you to imagine the nuclear level of any object.

Spirituality and purpose

The day without moving towards your purpose is, day without living, we all live to fulfill our needs as eating, parenting or even acquiring wealth for future, just like a bear acquired food for hibernation, but the moment, we are aware of our life purpose, and draw a path, we start living, but to get that moment, we need the science of spirituality, because spirituality establishes a bridge between your mind and soul, and due to which you will be able to discover and embrace your purpose of life via spiritual techniques such as meditation, mindfulness etc and not only declutch all the unnecessary ideas given by others into your mind, but also makes a connection with our self, which is more deep than ever,

This chapter goes with deep sense for the spirituality, and you may encounter outflow for the direction of the book, but to understand the topic I have to go deeper, because this book's one of the aims is to merge the eastern philosophy of spirituality with the western philosophy of entrepreneurship.

Steve jobs before changing the world came India, and learned many techniques like meditation and learned how to increase the human potential, listen to the inner voice etc due to which he was able to achieve so much, that no one can even imagine, as building the two most innovative companies which revolutionized the industries, in which they belongs (Apple changed the information age, and PIXAR changed the animation industry), most people wants to be like him, but nobody wants to do the boring work which is necessary for his vivid success, people who are so much enlightened, don't even care for their awards they just love and enjoy their work, because they are born to do this on earth and they know it, spirituality is the way to find your purpose too.

Spirituality and entrepreneurship

This book's main aim is to make you aware of future age, as well as establish a connection between spirituality and entrepreneurship, and gives you a great sense of life filled with joy, as basic idea is, entrepreneurship is all about solving a problem with your creative ideas as well as greater human potential to execute it, and spirituality is all about establishing the connection of you with yourself, and because of spirituality you will be able to take life at its up most level, where without external factor your heart will filled with joy and many super powers will be acquired which you can use in your day to day work, and due to this connection to your soul as well as your callings for this world, and you will be able to draw your purpose, merging with the knowledge and awareness of new age and powers from old school of spirituality, create solutions and live purpose driven life with full potential, achievement and joy in heart.

Indeed some people have god gifted abilities, which have made them billionaires or game changers like super analytics of warren buffet or boldness of Richard Brandson, or genius of Elon Musk but we all have one thing, which can increase our potential which is spirituality, from stone age, evolution of man, his religion, his tools and his lifestyle has occurred, but one thing remain same which is the concept of spirituality. However purpose to practice spirituality has changed as before humans do spiritual practice to please their god, and now people practice spirituality to increase their soul energy, and even for some it's to increase potential and work effectively and efficiently.

I believe everyone has a beautiful mind and vivid imaginative, by the influence of information age, due to which anyone can create the masterpiece in arts, science etc. but to make your mind up to maximum potential and utilizing this amazing age, and to be a contributor in the another age, you need embrace the power of spirituality, as following in the chapter you will notice different science and topics which are gathered for you from all around the world and arrange in the comprehensible form, due to which you can understand the topic of spirituality, and aware its power and potential. Also, you can start by picking 2-3 of them, and start the most amazing and joyful journey which not only makes you a better person or a contributor but also makes you a great entrepreneur.

I will go deep into this subject for the fact that all of us have least reach to the subject and from this chapter, which provides some insights and knowledge into modern way, you will be able to visualize the spirituality, and due to which the chances are you will adopt the path of spirituality for yourself, your career and most important for your spirit and ultimately enjoy the joyful fruit of life.

Deep relation of entrepreneurship and spirituality:

Entrepreneurship is meant to create future, and for that you need to connect to yourself and finding yourself and goes deep down into you by the way of spirituality, because it will enable you to not even connect to your soul and makes you able to see the future around your purpose, but also gives you many powers in order to be a successful entrepreneur, powers like focus, peace, declutched, adversity quotient etc.

Practice spirituality ----→discover yourself + powers to act as superior human ----→finding your purpose ----→ develop yourself around your purpose statement ----→ increases mind capacity and creativity by spirituality ----→entrepreneurship.

Brain vs. soul

All of us are living in a story our brain has created by the influence of other people, knowledge we have, and the perception we have created for our happiness, for example people in the stone age, wished for health, where as now people's happiness is wealth, as all are perceptions and situations into which we molded our emotional state, but there are two types of truths and happiness, one is the situational and subjected on the basis of perception and situation, and another is eternal truth which is the truth, of a soul, for example, people in earlier centuries used to say that earth is flat, but by the power of science, human curiosity and exploration

31

new perception is created, as the shape of earth is sphere, as science created a situation and we perceive the truth, but there is eternal truth of life which is 'eternal spirit', we created perceive truth by our brain which is only a part of the body run by our spirit, but by the time usage of brain becomes very high, which made this part of body so powerful that it rules us completely even to our souls, and due to which, we can't find the eternal truth of spirit or god, like education in science makes our brain stronger and logical, same as practice of spirituality makes our eternal truth more stronger, as spirit should govern us not our brain, that's why in the age of innovation where an innovator is the king, we need the power of our spirit to work on full potential because, as we feed our soul by spirituality our soul feed us and takes us to the right direction, we need to go for this life with full potential otherwise you will be crushed by either competition or mediocrity.

Just like truth, we also have two types of happiness, which is perceived and eternal happiness, perceived happiness is again is drawn out when we satisfy the story created by our brain, but there is another truth, whose frequency of joy, is much higher than the first one and most of us in our whole life experience, very little of it, because of our own peace activity which you will get to know later, so to move forward you need to adopt power of spirituality and makes stronger your brain as well as your soul.

New age powers from old schools:

Present moment awareness
When awareness of the surroundings are utmost, and all your mind potential is used in present moment it is called present moment awareness, which gives very high potential and ecstasy feeling. Living is present moment is taking charge of your brain by your spirit, but the fact is we all develop our mind so well, that our mind uses us, and all our life decision are decided by it only, but if we make our soul so strong that our soul dominates the powerful organ mind for seeking of god given path (which is often hindered by brain vibration), our soul can be strong by meditation and

mindfulness(observing mind activity) and also by educating ourself for the most important topic of spirituality. In western societies, which claim to have great universities and education system, even adopted this eastern concept of spirituality.

Joy of present can be experience by your own past experience, as you go back to your memories feel, the riskiest or dangerous activity you have done, whether it is driving car with high speed or climbing mountain or any other activity, to the pleasure activity of doing sex or smoking etc, all these activities force you to come into the *now* moment, that's why people are addicted to it, but via spirituality, that present moment joy and potential can be feel, to practice the concept there is also another motivation factor, to practice it, which is professionalism, consider a movie 'Sherlock Holmes' in which you always get fascinated by his great observing power (which he developed over time) and the good news is, you also can be Mr. Holmes in your own field, whether it is business or writing or marketing job, for example consider you are an entrepreneur and in your venture you faced a distribution problem but within a blink you generate a brilliant idea and you are shocked how can you generate such an idea, this euphoria moment of generating blink idea is the power of living in the present moment, within that blink you were living in the moment, in which you are highly creative as you aside the past-future and emotional mess, and order your brain to generate idea.

Also living in present moment increase your consciousness of surroundings and due to which, your self-esteem becomes high, and you will be able to work in assertive behavior as win-win condition in which you not only perform the task at optimum level but also able to win the hearts.

Benefits of the concept:
1) Sherlock Holmes power of great observing skills
2) Joyfully life
3) Great productivity and focus to do complex work with just blink of the ideas
4) Clarity

Methods to achieve the present moment awareness
Passive methods
1) Meditation,
2) Mindfulness (observe your mind)
3) Reading in the morning for few minutes to hours any spiritual article or book so that your soul becomes strong and drive your life.
4) **Correct your biochemistry:** food which increases your oxygen level, high energy and alertness for high focus to the brain.
5) **Resolving the concept of past and the future**: We are intelligent being and we have great memories but due to lack of self-education, and lack of learning attitude we take our bad experience as thinking blockers, and make a dent on our own belief system, so because of our own lack of awareness, we often give power to our experience, to create our future, so two ultimate activities you need to work on is, first for the past is having learning attitude from our experience and acquire the wisdom, and another is to have a great belief and hope for success for future, which will not make you always in future projections and anxious behavior, and you will live in present moment.
6) **Declutching**: it means reducing the substances around you which you do not use, it will gives you enormous amount of peace and joy, In Japan, people have the science, and ritual to clean up their surrounding and throw away all the in necessary things for peace.
Active methods
1) Observe your breath for few seconds (observing it going in and out from your lungs).
2) Think of your current situation and how can you improve it or make it better or what optimum activity you can do now, to realize the power of living in present moment fully.
3) Peppermint chewing gum: it might be sound crazy but chew the gum helps lot of people to focus and concentrate, again there are many tips in the world but you need to try everything and choose the best things for yourself.

Live like a lotus

This phenomena for living like a lotus, is the mindset created by adopting the path of spirituality, which gives you pleasure of still and clear mind, and you will be able to see the world as heaven, and even people throw critics on you, but your true colors will be the same just like mud washed away from lotus, live like the lotus means roots connected within mud, like world where selfish people created the hell or mud like environment, but rather than be like them you chose to have the mindset above. As people often stuck in the negative emotions created by their negative self, as greedy, selfish, arrogance, but with this concept, you will be able to soothe emotions and actually live like a lotus; this mindset is acquired by the following activities:

1) Involve much with spirituality: read, listens to spiritual content and try to comprehend them even in the beginning it looks like hypothetical but try hard to comprehend the spiritual literature with open minded approach.

2) Try to see the world with the spiritual content you have acquired.

3) Be aware of all your negative emotions and self.

As shown in figure power of spirituality, helps you to live like a lotus and makes you a better person, however, many people will argue that greed is good, but in the age of innovation when you stick to your callings for this world, then rewards will be enormous and your lotus mindset will give you more than your greed, there are mud emotions and lotus emotions, even in the long run lotus mindset, will pay you more reward and even gives you the energy of patience, late but huge rewards, and by the power of spirituality you can move from the mud to lotus.

As Mud emotions are:

1) Selfish
2) Greed
3) Dishonesty
4) jealousy

And after by the power of spirituality gives you mental state like

1) humble
2) love and care
3) Gratitude
4) Integrity

Although all the mud emotions are sometimes necessary for living, as human race because of passing lots of competitive phase like world war and slavery and to survive in this phase it is sometimes necessary to use negative emotions to go upward, for example for a poor man with family will find difficult as not to be greedy and fulfill his family need simultaneously, but the fact is after having some financial security people should go towards lotus mindset because it's the way of living, in which, you will fulfill your aim with peace and full potential.

CREATIVITY AND SPIRITUALITY

Humans are the only creatures, who has developed spirituality in them, which is in my opinion is happiness or peace of mind, feeling of god, rather than another animals, humans not only uses their senses, but also are able to enjoy them, as you can be pleased by perfumes via nose, music via ears etc, but next generation of pleasure, created by humans are pleasure of creativity, which can be developed over a period of time (which also can be called as pleasure of work), creativity is directly proportional to the happiness, and true state of happiness comes from peaceful mind, which comes from practice of spirituality.

There are many ways to practice spirituality, and most common and easiest way is, meditation in which, mind only thinks about one object, and object should give peace to the mind, example ocean waves (object depends on person to person), some imagine 'Buddha', as based on the mindset or emotions, projected by the object onto us, to make the session of meditation more effective use isolation earphones to avoid noise of surroundings and at least think of up to 5 minutes in the beginning , also to increase creativity one should try some yoga moves for example 'Aloom-Villom'

Practice of spirituality not only increase your performance in every role as human being but also clear your mind to see what actually you are born for, as mention earlier creativity comes from true happiness/peace of mind and if you practice spirituality, your mind and heart will be clear and you will be able to understand what your soul is saying to you, or what your heart demands from you (not others demands from you) and when you start fulfilling your true demands of life, then you start enjoying life in form of enjoying creativity.

By the practice of spirituality, we will be able to make future world as heaven because spirituality gives peace and happiness, creativity and satisfaction due to which just like Facebook viral, I hope spirituality viral will occur and by satisfaction level of the world increases less crime will be there and eventually world will be like heaven. I don't know whether it is true or not, that an organization of super intelligent people called 'Illuminati' whose members are trained at Indian secret school in Himalaya, where they learn spirituality to live their highest potential life(sources former Illuminati members interviews) and act as super human, by amplify the god given gift to human i.e. thinking capability and creativity., if a person knows his purpose of life then he/she has a potential to live like a legend, but purpose comes from inner self of an individual and to listen what inner self is saying to you, you must clear your invisible path which is connecting brain and heart which is done through spirituality that's why many legends of different nations practice spirituality, Practice of spirituality over time, you will find yourself up to a higher level when you will be able to connect to the god/cosmic energy/nature (partially), due to which, you will get the high-level ideas for you, your profession etc,.

In "Geeta" (holy book for Hindus), there is a concept of karma, when a person goes through path of spirituality he or she get rid of the good or bad karma, which is perception made by him/her, but after crossing all the chakras (even partially), an individual is able to see things clear, insightful and do things he is meant to do, and for what he has come on to this planet. To make this point a more multicultural context, let's take an example of a samurai, once the master of a samurai is killed by a person, so its samurai's duty to kill that person, for 2 years he was searching to kill him, then when the moment came up as samurai found him in a cave where he was hiding, samurai took his sword and aim his tinted blade towards his heart, via his chest, but just before samurai cut his heart, the person spit on samurai's face, samurai took his blade off him and went back, then this person asked the samurai 'why you are not killing me, I gave you enough reasons to kill me' samurai replied 'I was after you to kill you because of my duties but when you made me angry by spitting on my face you made my karma interfered and you entered my anger with my karma, and after soothing my emotions I will come back and will kill you'.

Seven chakras and creativity

In path of spirituality, there is a concept of 7 chakras needs to be achieved for salvation, but in current scenario, to live life to full potential they can be partially achieved, by practicing them in meditation you will be able to be highly creative, your creation won't be from any of the weak emotions of human being, but from the cosmic energy of the nature, it is said by many creative people, that ideas are free flowing in the nature, it's your mind to catch them, but after analyzing deeply about these chakras, karma and creativity it can be concluded that, 7 chakras can be used for profession, personal and spiritual reasons depend on the desperation of the individual in particular area.

7 chakras from the beginning are

1) ***Earth Chakra:*** First chakra, can be open by letting go your fear, in meditation think all of your fears, and then letting go by thinking the root cause of your fear and think that, fear is a perception made by your brain and fear is governed by human emotions and spirituality is above mind as 'no mind state'.

2) ***Water chakra:*** After overcoming your fear next is your desires, pleasure, and the process to overcome them as think of them feel them letting them go.

3) ***Fire chakra:*** This chakra is blocked by your anger, and blockage can be penetrated via thinking(same as above)

4) ***Heart chakra:*** Love, compassion,etc., many people will strike here because they are educated and brought up in a way that love means everything to them and above it, is nothing but spirituality, is above all due to which, this feeling need to pass on to connect with the ultimate cosmic energy which we are made of.

5) ***Throat chakra:*** Denotes intelligence, creativity as this article is based on creativity and spirituality, but if we talk about only creativity from the potential of your mind only then this chakra state is sufficient, but for those who wants to connect with the ultimate cosmic energy and feel creativity or receiving ideas from the nature, then you need to go beyond your intelligence and move towards another chakra.

6) ***Eye chakra:*** Psychic energy, intuition, many people feel its last state, but because they are overwhelmed from their intuition and subconscious mind, but you need to overcome this chakra, as after awareness of these chakras and feeling, you will be able to work on them easily, though meditation and mind fullness and you will be able to open the last chakra which is

7) ***The crown:*** After open this chakra you will be able to catch up the ideas from nature and your creativity will be seen as god gifted by other people For example aircraft, internet etc, as 2 centuries ago they could be treated as god energy but it was there already the waves, the aerodynamics,etc., just the comprehension level was not there.

This concept maybe hypothetical in nature for some people, but you can't understand this before doing it. The connection between your cosmic and the nature cosmic energy can be visualized, as think of a magnetic lines and its direction from down to up, same like your meditation posture and cosmic energy flows from your body via 7 chakras to up and feeling of god is achieved, and a person can be called enlighten, 'Buddha', this concept is helpful in creativity, by open your mind, to catch the ideas from the nature, try this concept and be open minded about the concept, as it has the potential to change your life.

Cleaning up your 7 chakras:

For better working you need to clean your chakras and the technique is, fill the bucket dip your legs, till your calf and thigh joint, for five minutes, and then throw this water into the toilet without looking at it.

Perceived and self-human

ı   Most of the world's population is perceived human, we perceive most of the thinking from our surroundings only, For example our habits, our reactions, even our careers, but in this topic I want to make you aware which I observe a lot in human beings and which I think nobody are aware of from childhood. We acquire all of our things from our surroundings, for example when loud parents have a child, it is more likely that from his childhood, he or she will react loud, but in this Information Age, and availability of literature, we are more aware, and because of spirituality we are able to adopt our self but we need to be aware, as much as we can, to find our self and also practice spirituality, which help you to link yourself with the data you acquire for yourself, here message is simple the way of life is by your true self which will come out by two powers i.e spirituality and awareness, awareness of things you perceive and spirituality to draw out your true self.

Enlightenment and Entrepreneurship

Enlightenment in my understanding, is having a state of mind or self and feeling of wisdom along with joy of peace, which gives you enormous happiness, the happiness which you can't find by materialistic things, but for those who haven't experienced it, will think it's waste, but again make a view for this way of life, after experience or at least try it with open-mindedness.

Imagine a person had financial troubles in his early life, due to which, he developed subconsciously a hunger for money and start working for it, he worked very hard day and night due to which he was able to become a wealthy person in his society, and along this journey he gave up many things for the money, but on the last day of his life when he was at the hospital waiting for the death, someone asked him 'did you enjoy the life you had, and his reply was just I wasted my life for money only', but if he had the wisdom and was somewhat enlighten, then he might change the last statement of his life, entrepreneurship is creating values for the customers which an entrepreneur will do best if he has sense of enlightenment, in the journey of achievements you also move with peace and joy of life, your enlightenment won't only serve you but also serve the people associated with you, due to which, if you apply your enlightenment in the entrepreneurship, you not only do the things which are necessary for the society and able to build ethics in business but also able to promote social entrepreneurship.

Modern ways to enlighten

In our previous ages, people used to have only few ways to enlighten and all nations have their own ways to get to this state, for example, Buddhism itself has many ways like meditation, chanting etc, but due to the information age, we able to merge the science from different nations and present it to you the basic information on how to start the way of enlightenment, in the modern era, we are deeply focused on materialistic world and the spirituality got vanished slowly, but thanks to our gurus and holy books by which we still able to keep in touch with this very art of life.

During our stay on earth, because of lack of awareness, we fulfilled only our materialistic needs, which emerged from our physical, emotional (body related needs) needs, but there is also most important need for human, which is need of your soul and due to its unmet supply, the end stage of life feels empty even achieved much materialistically.

With modern technology of information, sharing a wisdom is easy, by which you can try all and pick up the techniques, as per the suitability and make your own way to spirituality, and fulfill the need of soul, feeding of spirit is necessary, because when we die, we can't take the materialistic things with us such as name, fame or money as your soul after leaving the body won't care about your noble prize or big money, but will care about the activities you have done for your soul.

There are many ways for feeding your soul which are:

1) Peace activity
2) Meditation, mindfulness
3) Chanting
4) Philosophy

Peace activity:

Just like the eureka moment, we encounter when we discover or imagine something new (which can be inward as well as outward in nature), likewise there is the peace moment for your spirit too, in which you feel glimpse of enlightenment within yourself, a feeling of lonely peace which is out of the world, and this feeling is done by many different activities and based on person to person who resonate with the activity which can be from scuba diving to running(identification is you will feel your soul fulfilled) , some of the examples of these spiritual or peace giving activities are

1) YOGA
2) Running or swimming or simple brisk walking
3) Listening or reading spiritual things
4) Your own peace activity which can be varied and wired as from writing to smelling to underwater diving

As you begin your own spiritual journey you need to be fully alert to collect the data from your experience and record it in your journal, what are the activities which gives me peace or even disturbs me.

Meditation and mindfulness

These are the activities makes you connected with your soul and by the time you know about meditation and mindfulness, and gradually increase your time with these activities, you start feeding your soul, both of the activities has significant role in our life, just like a plant fill water in its fruit, as same as meditation and mindfulness feed our soul, and if done properly can have the potential to make our life joy full even in the adverse situations, and will also develop great materialistic qualities, like anti-fragile or critical thinking.

Mindfulness:

Observe your thinking and questioning it, or observe your brain activity by questions, like why I am thinking like that and so on.

Chanting

It may sound nonsense, but many people in both of the region, western and eastern claim that via chanting of some mantras, helped them achieve enlightenment, In chanting, as many religious books has their own mantras, and you should go for them only after resonating the content of the holy book you like, and then try mantras, as in our Hinduism, chanting of mantras, which are the language of god and uses to communicate with the god, just like code is used for communicating with machine.

Again this book provides many ways to succeeds in various aspects of life, and it's your suitability for picking up the technique so I would advise you to try all and pick according to your own satisfaction, from result of conducting all these activities

The most famous mantra is from 'Nichiren Buddhism' "Nam-myoho-renge-kyo"

Chant this mantra several times in the early morning and late night before sleep and find your suitability with the spiritual activity.

Philosophy

This way of enlightenment is from the philosophical books as the more you read philosophical articles, or listen to them, and examine various great philosophers as from Greece to Germany to India and develop your own philosophy, which is generated by creativity and this creativity, which is triggered by diversity of great philosophical data from different nations, and after submerged into it, and have love for it, you will be able to feed your soul by your developed philosophical mind.

Developing philosophy with healthy psychology

when you have a healthy psychology, you start forming your own frameworks for life, career etc, by awareness of worldwide literature, spirituality and etc, and this framework is developed eventually over time and make your unique philosophy for yourself, and move towards liberation state of soul, because after understanding the human existence, you move above it just like animal soul moves towards human soul according to Hindu philosophy, this concept can be perceived as mere hypothesis but there is a scientific benefit by developing philosophy, As Tony Buzan said we only retain only 5% of what we read after two weeks, but once we made our own philosophy on anything, we likely use the knowledge we acquired much, as we retain it, develop the philosophy by it and develop our intellect and life.

A man has to develop a healthy psychology, with the help of 7 chakras and mindfulness concept of spirituality, by which, your high level philosophy will be developed as you acquire more knowledge.

Entrepreneurs the future saints:

In India or other Asians countries, you can find monks, saints, who has devoted all their life to god, but the fact is, spirituality is like ecstasy feeling and because of this ecstasy feeling they left their homes and all the comfort of urban, this ecstasy in western literature is called as flow states, in the history and books of Hindu religion(which are written thousands of years ago like Vedas) has lots of inventions written including aerodynamics, living cells,etc., saints in Hindu religion, practice spirituality and able to access a lot of brain area to understand and develop science, but lack of comprehension and ignorance to these literature, we unable to use them, due to which we invented some of these technology in just hundreds of years ago, by the use of our ordinary mind state, but in the next age people has to adopt the path of spirituality in order to find their purpose (which is mainly to create value) for others with the inner inspiration empowers by power of spirituality and also work in four times more productive manner.

Just like in animal kingdom, there is a categorization on the basis of who will eat to whom, where king is lion, likewise in our world, there is a categorization of the basis of contribution by an individual to the world and where entrepreneurs are the modern age kings, like saints were in thousands of years ago, as saints was believed had the potential, due to which they were (some are still) called the upper level humans because of their mental capability, In India or other Asians countries you can find monks, saints who devoted all their life to god, but the fact is increase in spirituality is like ecstasy feeling, due to which they left their homes and all the comfort of urban, this ecstasy in western literature is called as flow states.

This universe is made of the ultimate cosmic energy which

we all know as the god and our soul is a part of it, and which is our main source of energy which is above all (brain and body) and spirituality is the way to connect the ultimate energy so in layman terms practicing of spiritual activities like meditation, mindfulness,etc. with the mindset of inclination of your soul to the ultimate cosmic energy, so by power spirituality anyone can be a great contributor or king or modern saint.

Innovation age and spirituality:

We all are connected to each other and due to information age, we have even power to connect to the whole world, but we forget to connect with most important person, 'to our self' and spirituality will help you to connect to our self, materialistically it will help you to have clear thoughts, peaceful mind, which you can use in decision-making, and also help you to alter your thinking capability.

CHAPTER 4

Personal Development for Innovation Age

Evolution occurred in various field in science and technology, but there is also an area in which people are associated in every age which is area of personal development and also with the evolution of ages, the evolution in science of personal development have also evolved, with the merging of neuron-chemicals and bio-chemicals along with psychology and other human aspects, the new age science of development is evolving at greater rate and the glimpse of it is shown in this chapter.

Personal development should be the area of concern for every one because in the next age the greatest assets is you, not your wealth or wealth generating assets you have created, because in the long run it's you and your development which will matters the most and your capability to acquire and generate the other assets (physical or intellectual), Also if you have the kind heart and want to help others, just help yourself first by this great science of personal development and in long run you will be able to help others directly or indirectly and for self help the biggest tool is personal development, Personal development helps you become a bold, intellectual and a confident contributor for the world.

This section personal development is divided into 4 parts and all the parts are essential for the personal growth and development and first two are the framework as well as techniques to enhance the strengths and management styles, which will enables you to closely see the world with different angles and on the basis of this framework you can have much open mindedness in observing and dealing with the world along with your inherent style of dealing and managing people(awareness of which will give you a clear idea in managing people) , third are the motivational techniques, and the last one will provide great insights for some of the main factors which directly influence the work and success in anything we do, so the flow of the section of personal development is going from framework for strengths and human resource management, reinforced with key factors of success to techniques, empowers by the motivational techniques.

This section has 4 key areas:
1) The seven key strength of an entrepreneur
2) Management style
3) Key areas of consideration for success
4) Motivation Techniques

The seven key strengths of an entrepreneur:
Entrepreneurship is the mindset to change the world into better and if we are concerned about personal development, we need to acquire the mind set of entrepreneurship, for example Elon Musk when he discovered the urgency for control over pollution he invested in the company, Tesla, as transportation is a necessary part of human life and we can't stop the automobile industry to grow, as it essential to human life, but we can eliminate the exhaust system; exhausts carbon monoxide and other harmful gases which directly affects us and the nature in the form of global warming, and replace it with the electric car concepts, Elon with his entrepreneurial mindset has a vision to be a proactive for the issue of pollution and promoted the concept well enough that his efforts took the company from the hell of bankruptcy to the hot stock price company in the share market and made many investor millionaire and himself a billionaire, even he does not care much about money, because of his pure entrepreneurial mindset(mindset is best

explained in spirituality section in lotus mindset).

Entrepreneurship is great way of life with bold aim; in which you are taken out the things internally and all work is drawn on the basis of personal development, due to which, I bound entrepreneurship and personal development as the key factor for success.

The seven key areas are:
1) Focus
2) Creative thinking
3) Risk taking capability
4) Confidence
5) Determination
6) Knowledge acquisition
7) Networking

Even though all the strengths are somehow connected to each other but to make a framework, I have illustrated them in seven for the sake of better comprehension and judgment of our self and others, awareness of every strengths in yourself, will give you a better picture of question of why (why I am not successful or why I am not a better entrepreneur), Some of the strengths in us are high while some are low, however you need all of them to be able to succeed. In this section, there are some techniques for acquiring strengths, as I believe that your success depends on your strengths, so you need to improve on your weaker strengths, make them stronger. For instance, if you have 3 strong strengths which includes focus, knowledge acquirer, creative thinker and low in the 4th one which is "risk taker". You need to make sure you improved on your weaker strength, as having all the strong four strength will move you forward to positive moment. let's take real life example of warren buffet before acquiring some of the strengths he was nothing but after acquiring all the strengths he started growing with pace and in a place of world's rich category as he acquire all the other strengths from a book which develop him personally.

So let's get started

1) Focus

It is the most important thing you need to work on even before you work on your purpose of life. Consider a spring and then compare it to human life as when you gave energy to the spring it will deviate as per energy given to it; life is like that without the power of focus.

Now consider bow and arrow in which with the power of focus your life which is spring is converted to bow and arrow in which you give energy to the bow string and aim the arrow by the power of focus to your goal and when you leave both the object in bow and arrow, you will likely get to your goal and get to heights in the life whereas in spring when energy is over it come back to his original position.

So now, the question is how can you have great focus like Sherlock Holmes?

1) Meditation: it's an art which might be boring but will help you to connect to your inner self

2) Live in the present moment: we either live in past or future but if we will learn how to live in present moment, you can become Sherlock Holmes in your own field

2)   Creative thinking

This strength is rather most important in terms of entrepreneurship, as bringing creative solutions for the problem is itself the major role of an entrepreneur, not only in entrepreneurship but rather in any field nowadays. Creativity is an essential part of humans and it differentiates us from other animals. I believe that we maybe same in biochemistry or emotions but idea generation is something we have own moments(because we have our own knowledge and experience); some people have eureka moments from simple actions like reading, relaxing in warm water or watching educational video, while others have very wired circumstances for their creativity for example Japanese inventor *Yoshinaro Nakamatsu* and many great Korean inventors claimed of their great creativity moments occurred, while they are in deep water and stay there just before death moment, one thing you can do all the time is to cultivate the habit of acquiring knowledge because knowledge is the basics of creativity.

Basic techniques to develop your creativity:

Invest in yourself

As this is main weapon in the next age is you; thus you need to develop yourself as well increase your creativity by learning different skills and reading different articles on various topics which will make you creative by means of diverse knowledge.

Learn to be happy

Have you ever notice why a child is always happy--- because he is always learning and just like we enjoy and makes our self happy by fulfilling the luxury need of all our senses, same as our creative sense need to be fulfilled by luxury of learning. Happiness and creativity are directly proportional to each other; when you are happy you become highly creative and when you are creative you have eureka moments which makes you happy. A hack for this, Just like inverse action hack our biochemistry, you need to learn to be happy to be highly creative, psychologically unhappy by any external situation created, which highly impose our perception, due to psychology our biochemistry of the body changes and our body language shows the result (sad posture), but if you are aware of it and uses action to change biochemistry by changing our body posture indirectly to happy posture (by holding pen between teeth etc or any happy posture you will be able to be happy).

When you learn how to be happy and learn your own happy moment creations you can use them for being creative so next time you become sad think that it's unprofessional.

Travel

Travelling has the major effect to the individual's creativity because by traveling to different nations, he or she encounter different culture and different ideas as well as different people, thus he/she learn something from this diversity and diversity increases creativity

Vocabulary and creativity

Language is really a greatest invention of man, which not only helps to convey ideas in the form of literature but also able to growth various fields such as arts, science etc., language is also helpful in making you highly creative because of its vocabulary. English language is indeed the most popular language in the world, because this language consists of words which were taken from different origin of the world, for example from India, Greece or in French, someone invented or discover something and name it in their language and simultaneously English language took it in its collection of words, coming to the creativity and vocabulary link, as when we encounter a new word and read its meaning then our brain captures a diverse words which made your brain imagine about the word and simultaneously increases the creativity by practice of imagination as well as collecting a new and diverse knowledge for your creativity.

Supplements

We have two different entities: body and mind. We always think and do about body but success is dependable on your mind only. Think of it, you and Steve Jobs have same body and biochemistry of the body but the difference is he do a lot for his mind which includes fasting to detoxify the body and make great thoughts with only good chemical of the body, if we work on our mind food we will be able to think better and feel better and do best every day, there are few brain supplement for the brain which are mainly herbal and easily available in the market in form of vegetables and herbal supplements,

They are:

1) Ginkgo balboa
2) Brhami(HINDI WARD)
3) Broccoli
4) Sugar
5) Dark chocolate
6) Ginger

There are also other types of supplements for the brain but I want to mention one discovery here that our brain has muscles which are responsible to acquire these supplements, but there are brain supplements which your brain don't absorb, that's why in brain supplement industry customers reviews are very different from each other, as same supplement absorb in your brain might not work in your friend's brain, just like digestion of food depends upon your blood group and your food. So try and make a list of the supplements which your brain absorbs the most so that you can make good use of your food to draw creative work.

3)   Networking and relationship building

If you are a genius, but you don't know how to make friends and make great relationships, you won't be able to execute your idea or talent, because one brain can't influence much in society but if you know this skill you can influence the world with the power of other people too, it is proven that materialistic happiness (above 80%) is based on connectedness with other people (success story of Facebook), you can acquire this skill by the following exercises:

1) Do not make relationship with the aim of using others, otherwise the relationship is not going to last. Make friends with the aim of sharing your strengths to create something good.

2) Be open-minded and interact with first approach.

4)   Confidence

It is the strength which has the potential to makes you anti fragile and can have high adversity quotient, we all know deep about confidence so I won't go deep into it, but I will provide you some insights to how confidence can be increase:

1)   Have a strong belief system in yourself: with the strong believe in yourself you can have great confidence.

2)   Great purpose of life: when you stick to your callings you won't suffer the lack of confidence even by others influence.

5)   Risk taking

Just because of lack of this ability many great ideas goes in to dustbin and just because of only this ability, even stupid ideas worked and gave great rewards to the individual, many of us are lacking in this capability because of our life style and its comfort, insecurities towards taking risk and negative mindset is created from influence of others, after close examination some creative insights of how this ability can be increases is drawn(I researched a lot for this), again all the data in the book are hypothesis and observations and like all other books it gives insights on various angles of life, to improve your life you need to have much of take away from this book, as this book gives you creative ideas.

How to increase risk taking capability

We have body muscles likewise we have brain muscles for different powers like focus, risk taking, courage, but due to circumstances we were brought up in; we develop and under develop these brain muscles and eventually powers, but at this age we are now more aware of all human strength, due to which we can know which strength I need to develop, which is not making me moving forward exponentially.

One is risk taking capability, Just like arms muscles, risk taking muscles also can be develop with both internal and external exercise, following are some examples of exercises for it.

1) Increase your biochemistry: Testosterone is responsible for lacking in risk appetite which can be increased by few activities from consuming fruits like watermelon, pomegranate, etc(eating herbal or even non veg to increase testosterone level) to change your actions like standing and holding your belt, always sit with open hands as dominant posture(power posing).

2) Feel like a lion: Visualize yourself as a lion.

3) Do the job which makes you fear: Everyday do an activity which makes you fearful by consider the end picture, which is developing your risk taking muscles and by visualize yourself first in that fearful situation and then try to solve it and face it intellectually and then do it which will eventually will increase your risk taking capability for your career.

4) Metabolism: The easiest way to test a man testosterone level is by saliva so if you chew a chewing gum (don't do it much) during a workout will also increase your t-levels.

This new age of development which is governed by the deep science of our body, in which we introduce external factors to our mindset to develop a certain habit or strength, as we all have almost same bio chemistry and neuron chemistry but because of our situations and critical incidents happened in our past days, but by the power of awareness of these science we are able to hack our internal systems by the governed factors of external stimuli, for example by introducing the above stimuli, anyone can hack his bio and neuron chemistry of the body as by generating more testosterone and endorphins, which helps in making person a risk-taker internally.

Remember you need to acquire data, test it and if it gives positive results apply it in your life and Write it in your journal.

6)   Knowledge Acquisition

Mahatma Gandhi once said "live as if you will die tomorrow, learn as if you will live forever", knowledge acquisition is directly linked to purpose and creativity of a person, just like body building is only done when the individual has a passion or reason to build; likewise knowledge acquisition takes place if you have passion for your purpose and creativity, then your mind will work in automatic mode for knowledge acquisition and the more you acquire the knowledge and skills, even high ambitions for oneself is even a great purpose of life which creates a hunger for knowledge within you.

Some straight forward ways to install this automatic program of knowledge and skills acquisition within you are:

1) Have great sense of purpose and develop your own purpose of life.

2) Increase your creativity and have passion to create something.

7)   DETERMINATION

Determination is the strength of never giving up and live with your purpose of life, determination of a person is not checked by his situations of success (everyone behaves with high determination in success situation) but rather checked in state of failure, because in failure situations your true self is comes out from inner self and shows how developed you are, your determination checked best in adverse situations, the determination can be developed and few points are:

1) Worst case scenario, in which if you look in your decision every possible outcomes, from high success to worst case, because when you are aware your worst outcome then this will not hit your determination.

2) Awareness of your true ambitions and you won't hit by your failures, but will learn from them and keep motivated by your callings in the world.

Leadership and Management

Due to our core strengths and weakness we develop our own unique way to deal with the surroundings, but we sometimes confuse to use our own ability to deal and manage people, (because of the influence of others) and this makes us in a position of weak human management skills, but if we really want to lead (as more you develop your god giving way of manage people, the better the leader you will be), this section gives you a better idea and makes you aware of all the four management style, people uses which resonate with their strengths and by further developing your management style you can become even great leader too.

So the four management styles are
1)   Networking
2)   Thinking
3)   Achieving
4)   Influencing and convincing

As these management style is drawn out after observing lots of people around the world and due to which you can aware and find your own style of managing the most important resource (human resource is the most important resource in the world consider example of Instagram or Whatsapp had only few employees but these employees made billion dollars company).

Networking management style:
The outgoing, friendly, great communication skills has this

style of managing people, their charisma itself let them lead others, because of their nature and helping heart, people always listen and ready for them to help so this style is rather happy go lucky kind of style in which the individual has many friends and these friends never let them down, even employees always ready to work for them with the ease of friendliness in their boss.

Thinking
The individual who likes interpretation of data and wanted to be aware of current situation, these people likes to know everything better than the other due to which they lead others with their knowledge and strategy, also they are good learners and like to learn as many things as they can.

Achieving style
These people can't feel good, unless they achieve their desired goals, these people are often fast decision makers and eventually develop their acumen in their own fields, due to which people surround by them can't say no to them, because of their aggression and desperation to achieve something, they are good motivators and can give their high energy to others by their actions and wards.

Influencing and convincing
These people are highly aware of the strengths and weakness of them and others due to which they are able to influence the other people and manage them by power of influence.

Business skills and management style
Business is the one of the main part of our society and due to which many people involved in it, this topic aim is to link between management style and business skills and following is the linkage:

Thinking style: Strategic skills
Influencing and convincing: human resource skills
Achieving style: Business development skills
Networking style: Marketing skills.

Entrepreneurs and strengths

Four entrepreneurs has taken for their strength examination, these people, comparatively are of diverse personalities from each other from ruthless genius 'Steve Jobs 'to the very friendly and bold 'Richard Branson', from the diversified problem solver 'Elon Musk' to the stick to one field 'Elizabeth Holmes'.

Elon Musk

Let's start with the entrepreneur whose inspiration created our great superhero tony stark (iron man) and also inspires me and gives me the power to take bold decisions for my life and change the world, he is highly motivating character, billionaire and is worth examining for the seven strengths and management style, data taken from books and videos and examining well, Elon, before coming to USA had few strengths, only but after he started the journey, started to acquiring the strengths, his desperation to achieve the goal is more important than his comfort zone which changes his mental state and to acquire any kind of potential he needed to achieve high, (Robert Kiyosaki told in his book 'either you choose comfort or rich') after the success of his first venture elon acquired rest of the strengths and keep developing them, which enables him to move forward with speed of light and he entered in the field of solar energy, electric cars and even rocket science space x and make successful all of his unrealistic goals and ventures, he was able them to do is only on the basis of his personal development.

Elon is a great thinker and his thinking capability was sharpen by books he read all day and night in his childhood because he has the thinking management style in which he strategically runs all the companies.

About his developed strengths, he is a great creative thinker as he first solved the problem of yellow pages and banking and made the activity online which tells us he is a knowledge seeker and risk taker.

Elizabeth Holmes

Founder and CEO of theron(leading blood company) provide innovating solutions for great problems of blood testing industry, Holmes is a Stanford dropout, her inspiration was her uncle who died because of not diagnosed at an early stage cancer and because she had a feeling of can't do anything for her uncle and in early age she started the company, now she is a billionaire, like other contributors, she just want to change the world, as shown in figure her strengths she is more of strategic person and has the quality to see future and add her creativity into it and even a business person because she collaborate with the other companies to work on her core business and let them distribute for her.

Steve jobs

Everyone knows Steve and many people inspired everyday from him and still learning from him via videos and books, but it needs the heart to be a Steve jobs even rude to his employees but he has heart for the technology, with not much technical background, Steve have contributed a lot in information age and even in the transition into innovation age, because of the products and services of Apple Inc., people feel more deep the consequences of information age, I believe anything you do from heart touches the other's heart, his products are designed from heart with no loose ends and because even have high price than his competitors, Apple is one of the leading company a brand, talking about Steve's strength he also had a great vision for his company and product and because he is able to proactively design the products, has great sense of promotion, high speed with great focus but people with these abilities has to give up something because of focusing too much on the industry, he couldn't focus on his personal life and due to which he faced a lot of problems in his late twenties, he was very poor in relationship building and people stick to him because of his great sense of purpose.

Richard Brandson

He might be the boldest entrepreneur among us because he started almost 200 companies and start working in his teenage and even wrote some famous books, whatever he thinks he do, from trying to capture the impossible market share of coco cola and Pepsi by started a company called virgin cola to the field of aerodynamics, he is very adventurous and have tried the riskiest sports available in the world, among which he was about to die many times but still try them, many people says he is a lucky pig, but the main learning from his life is try to make boldest decisions as you can and do what your heart says, not what statics says, he believes in happy go lucky approach, in which you think that life is very short to fulfill your dreams and you need to take action, the fast you take decision the more experience you will have and the more growth will happen, and more develop in business decision and acumen, from the old sayings, there is a saying that the man who work without thinking or the man who only thinks gets no result, so you need to think and act for success but Richard's philosophy is you act you learn you act better.

Strengths and career position:

Whether it is industrial age or information age, the level of strengths in you shows your career position as well as your financial conditions, as you can see in the pictures of all four leading entrepreneurs has all the strengths with higher level due to which they are great leaders, but there was a time when they didn't have this much level of strengths, but as soon as they started their journey of life purpose, they not only increases their existing strength level but also generate new one's for the sake of their life purpose.

even yours life or career position is directly depends on these core strengths and your vivid imaginative purpose of life, so just like each entrepreneur above was giving rating for his each strength you can also make your own strength rating chart and improve them slowly.

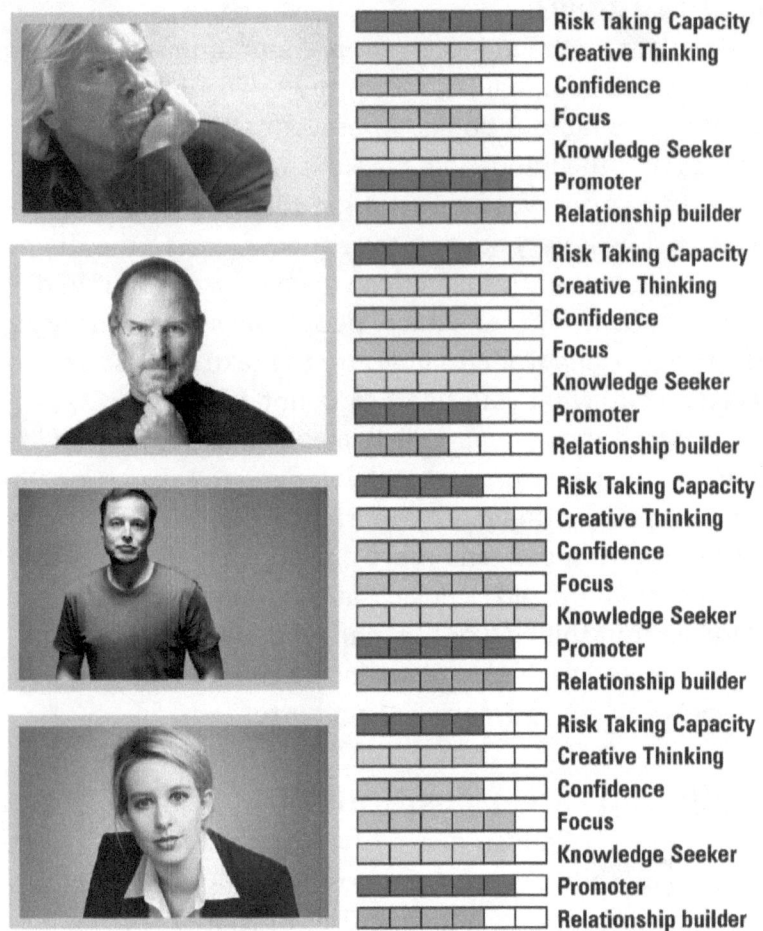

CHAPTER 5

Motivation

Motivation is the internal energy, which drives you for the life purpose path (to which everyone thinks and says impossible or irrelevant for you), to accomplish anything in life you need motivation, all the time this motivation level faded away, because of the surroundings and influence of others, you need to keep your motivation molecules always in exited state to fulfill your dreams, Donald triumph once was asked, how could you achieve so much in your life, to which he replied he daily feed himself with the motivation energy, by either read or listen to inspirational books or videos, which keeps him positive, enthusiastic and he was able to generate positive ideas, which helped him to get from the state of bankruptcy to billionaire position, Steve jobs once told to the students of Stanford about his dot theory, as before Apple there were the incidents that happened to him, due to which he was always feeling sad and think why this happened to me, but once he was able to connect all the critical incidents happened to him in form of dots after his success, then he concluded, everything happened to you, has to happened to you for better you, but many times in the god written path or your life purpose, we often find our self in the negative mind set or in discourage situations, and because the god written path blocked by your own negative ideas and we end up in giving up with the short term conditions (which is the only failure of life),but if you keep motivated yourself and inspired by find your own inspirational person or book or anything which touches your heart and motivates you deeply, by hitting your belief of your success and take off all the dust of other's influence (just like carpet is beaten by stick to blow off the dust), your probability for success will be much higher because motivation gives you energy to act and creative ideas to move forward, bodybuilders takes protein supplement which makes them not only able to lift the heavy weight but also to build muscles, same phenomena occurs here also as you need motivation dosage in order to achieve high in life.

Techniques for motivation and higher productivity

Wards and stimulation

A technique to sudden change in cognitions and energy to either achieve much or feel much, take a piece of paper or make a card board of wards contains the wards which excite you more about your passion for example 'entrepreneurship, creativity' gives positive energy to move forward with your life aim, you need a morning routine to just read them, and they open the blockage of cognition(blockage created by the influence of others) for your passion to execute, through passion ward nozzle, we have the power to change our cognition, emotions etc for our own benefits, our brain works on absorption and reflection things, we observe our surroundings and observe the vibes from it and reflect the same back, but what if we hack our system and let the brain absorb the things which gives us energy for our purpose through wards and reflect the passion for work back to the society, for example for me its entrepreneurship, leadership, picture of a great entrepreneur like *Elon Musk.*

Passion sound therapy

Reading increases creativity and makes an upper cognition level in you, whenever you read to a great leader, philosopher, thinker your brain start acquiring the thinking potential of the thinker you are reading the work of, same phenomena occurs in listening (even in mush effective way, that's why we have two ears), passion sound therapy works on the phenomena that, when we listen to any ward, we immediately form a picture or a imagination which impacts our cognition and makes it to think in a particular direction, some wards impact like a poison, some impacts are herbal for our purpose or passion, there are the wards or statements whose mental picture gives a great energy and motivation.

In this technique, we need to make our own journal of

wards (wards which makes a positive cognition), listen to them by either recorded voice of yours or listen on web, even music is also be the source of motivation consider the work of Hans Zimmer, whose composition is as motivating (combination of sound waves or energy decoded by our brain into motivation state or high energy and enthusiasm), same as NLP sound waves which give more concentration power, I was so crazy with the potential of sound energy that, was created a hypothesis that just like different music gives different response in our brain(slow relaxes you, trance music gives energy to you), imagine if we can create sound waves based on the profession of the person for example an architect's brain function differently from the business man and we create sound waves for the profession of architect to make him more productive same as for business man, investor, scientist etc.

Continuously searching your own motivational wards, music and listen to them on the daily basis is a great indirect source of energy, as sound energy decoded from our brain into motivation energy.

Active statement

'See yourself lying on the grave dead, now think about the regrets you have now which you wanted to do in your life', this statement may be familiar to you and you might heard of it earlier, but the fact is nobody is ever feel it and if feels, nobody continues for long, living their dreams and later after read the statement you no longer respond intellectually and emotionally, because your mind has already created the thoughts to make you lazy, because our mind function is to make our body comfortable or we can say just like when we contact to fire, a sensation is created and the brain order the body to get off from the area, likewise when we come across to these statements we first response emotionally, but soon or later your lazy or body comfortable phenomena gives birth to the thoughts to these statements as anti-respond for future, but spirit purpose is to make you move forward towards your life aim for what you are here, because if god wants you to live like animal and do nothing or contribute any creative work to the world, he

might send you as an animal, In Hindu philosophy and books it is written as 'we came from animal kingdom and crosses over 8400000 species then became a human', but many things we still have from them which makes us move backward like long nails etc, but if we increase the power of soul by spirituality, we might live our purpose, coming back to the topic we all have our own active statement(the statement which has the potential to awake you from your comfort intellection and move you towards your life aim).

Once in my college there was a seminar on the topic 'thinking today as last day of your life makes you more productive and aware of your life goal' , as the seminar move forward and all are agree with the statement, but then a Stanford professor who was there, argued that rather thinking it's the first day of life is more powerful statement, and I was thinking it is not the statement which is powerful, but the feeling or emotional response it gives to the individual, it depends on person to person to which statement makes the individual active or aware of life aim and so have your own active statement, because you are living in the innovation age, not in the animal kingdom, you need to be futuristic and ambitious in the way of life god has decided for you in order to survive.

Motivating figure resonates from your purpose

There are people who you admire the most and just after reading or watching these people, gives you a sudden great energy and motivation to do something in your life too, if you haven't have your own motivational figure then keep looking for them, because these are the people you resonates and get motivated and by their help you too can be like them, considering the fact that you need to build your own personality but for sake of motivation you need to choose your leader, for example, my own motivational leader is ELON MUSK every time I see any news or any video about him I feel energetic and gives me energy to move forward into my own path of life, so find your own leader, just like when we projected god wa made a picture or imagine the ultimate power of universe due to which just by imagine the power we code our brain to move forward with positive energy in life, likewise in career you need a career lord for the positive projections and inspiration to code your brain towards that big imagination.

Optimum cognition working

Consider a machine, working on optimum situations like accurate temperature etc and also operated by skilled operator, gives optimum results as well as can have a great life span and if anything is wrong with the machine it suddenly get checked and corrected by a technician, likewise human machine, as if our cognition is not at optimum level(maybe because of any reason for emotional problem or surroundings), then we not only make our decision wrong but also perform worst and because awareness of human machinery is needed, let's take this point with the help of 80/20 principle according to which our 80% profit comes from 20% of work, but if your cognition is at optimum level you will be able to work whole day with great efficiency and productivity, as consider yourself as machine for sake of success and excellence and use as many techniques to maintain your machinery at optimum level like cognitive therapy.

Important Notes

There is only one life and you can't afford to waste it on what others say about you, as nothing is impossible. consider your core strengths; if you think that they are very weak than anybody else then think again that he maybe into the personal development journey more than you, and it's ok if you lose today there is always another day.

I think that going to motivational seminars or watching motivational videos, creates a fake virtual positive imagination in you which are created by vivid words full of color and makes you drive for few weeks or few months but if you develop yourself and your purpose then you are more likely be in the auto pilot and these motivational videos will makes you accelerate in the desired direction, consider you are sitting in a car which is your mind and body and the resources you have but if you don't know where you need to go and aim at materialistic gains as luxury life etc., then you will more likely won't achieve it, but if you know your goal clearly you will utilize the car at top speed and accelerate much with these motivational speakers.

But your desperation is much higher than your negative defense system and you decided to strong your belief but you don't know what to do then.

One more technique to weak your own negative defense system by simple word "awareness" when you aware of your own mind negative function then you are giving hydrogen bomb to your belief system (belief of high ambition) to fight against negative defense system (which is making you halt due to comfort or fear) and as you work on yourself and overcoming these challenges you will one day fill all the leak points.

CHAPTER 6

Critical factors which are directly related to success

FLOW STATE

The ability of human beings to generate the creative idea with ease(feels like mind working without distraction), I believe everyone has their own flow state, the external environment (which is unique for everyone) merges with your diet due to which your biochemistry of the body is so aligned in you, that you able to generate the great idea with the help of the information you have just like connected the dots of information acquired by you consciously and subconsciously and use that data to generate a eureka moment and this eureka moment makes your productivity four times better.

Bio-chemicals responsible for the flow state are
1)   ENDORPHINS: Responsible for the high energy
2)   ANANDAMIDE: Lateral thinking
3)   DOPAMINE: Pattern recognition
4)   NOREPINEPHRINE: Alertness

Also these bio-chemicals can be align into optimal quantity in you, in order to give you in the flow state and this internal phenomena is governed by external environment which is unique for everyone, following are some observations you can apply to yourself:

1)   Brisk walking: You will find many great intellect and creative people has a schedule of early morning or post dinner walk, which is responsible for better alignment of these bio-chemicals

2)   Spirituality: The practice of spirituality not only gives you peace but also makes your bio-chemicals in optimal situation and this phenomena you act internally for example mindfulness, meditation etc., also spirituality also makeup the mind set which is helpful to accelerate the flow moment for example lotus mind set.

3)   Adventure sports: Many people observe that certain adventure takes them into the flow state.

EMOTION OF SUCCESS

You go to a party or meet someone, inspired by him, you got a feeling of doing something great in the life or make life more rich, you stick to this emotion till your lazy part enter and ruined your emotions and belief, but same belief had the potential to make you what you always wanted as *"the more desperation for success the more will be the success rate"*, you need to be strong and stronger belief because more your ambitions are there, the more belief in yourself required to achieve them. Many people don't dare to imagine big ambitions either because they don't have enough energy to see themselves up to a level (maybe they feel very comfortable in current life) and they don't need any change, in short, they don't have the drive, but few people dare to imagine but due to many leaks in their beliefs they failed to achieve it and spend life in anxiety and future and never feel the fruit of life but few people enjoys life with high satisfaction and fulfillment of high ambitions.

So let's get started with points for better understanding
Your story started with the adrenaline rush generated by the

ambitious emotion which sustain until a fight between your belief (having a better life or contribute great to the world) VS your negative defense system activated either by others people criticism or laziness and devil won and you have lost.

You need to know your path, your vision, your purpose of life, because I hope you know money is not the high ambitions (result of short term thinking), you see the interviews of billionaires, they treat money as a reward not the ambition. So if you are aiming for wealth then I must say you need a purpose because money can't buy you a deep happiness and only gives you fulfillment of your ego which won't last much, but money is the resource to create or to contribute to the world.

To know your purpose of life you can ask yourself various questions (which you also can find from web) like

- What I am good at?
- What are the things people ask you often?

And many more Along with your strengths

My advice is just make a journal for yourself and write all about you (many people think it's stupid or feel lazy, my advice is check your negative defense system) about your discoveries about yourself in critical situations.

Your strengths and passion by filling as many questionnaires from web as you can and write your purpose of life as per your knowledge and comprehension, for example say you have a strength of intellect and passion to teach and then along the way you made your life vision as my life aim is to change as many life as I can, (every teacher must think like that) but as you move with this purpose and stretch your strengths your purpose become much bigger now, you think to develop new science which will contribute to humans to a great extent and you now work on this more vivid vision which was made by taken action for your previous purpose, which stretched your strengths and make you able to lead a high satisfactory and rich life, wealth is a reward because in previous times due to lack of connectivity, great talents got hidden due to which talented people became poverty-stricken, due to miss location etc. This makes people more money minded due to which their aim became money and people became mediocre, but as we are humans and we can change our cognition from being money minded and greedy to acquire skills and nurture your talent based on your strengths. Believe me there is nothing joyful then to make contribution to the world by your stretched strengths.

Alexandra the great had a vision to win the world due to which he was able to almost win the whole world, all credit goes to his vivid imagination and strong belief as he was also a human just like you, same biochemistry flows in him, but the fact is he used his biochemistry for himself as positive chemicals secreted and made him stronger and creative, all done by sub conscious mind work for his strong belief.

As after you made a journal and living your purpose of life, you will automatically acquire skills and knowledge and the winner attitude to accomplish you dreams.

As the more vivid imagination of your dream is the more likely you will achieve, it may take time based on many variables as accurate time etc but success is inevitable

So practice two things to make your belief system stronger so that you can fight against your own negative defense system (which works against you).

Life is one and it is really very short to live.

The three techniques need to practice to fill the leakage are

1. Practice blocking negative thinking for whole one day once a every week and not let even one negative thought to come, In the beginning it will be very difficult just like meditation, but after you practice you will be able to achieve it.

2. Mindfulness: Every time you encounter any negative thought just remember it's your defense system not you and try to figure out by self questions like 'why I thought like that' 'is it fear of criticism or failure or poverty', if you think this fear is inevitable then manage it rather than give up your purpose.

3. Practice imagination of your dream or your high ambition at night or in the morning; try vision board etc kind of stuff.

Now after purpose you will automatically acquire self and field knowledge for your purpose but to make it easy, here are few topics you need to search for yourself:

    1. Emotional quotient, human quotient, happy quotient, adversity quotient.

    2. Self management: Like new techniques for self management, time management, handling critical situations by imagining yourself in the difficult situations under the domain of your purpose just like case studies and try to solve it.

    3. Self awareness: Like what time you become more creative or what is your blood group to see what food will give you more benefits and high energy, or what exercise makes you more active and which yoga Pose is great for you because energy means killing laziness.

    Now along the way you are acquiring more knowledge and increasing your potential and living joyful life, continuously update your purpose of life and keep going.

    Remember 10000 steps journey starts from step 1 so which ever level are you in as long as you move forward you will succeed.

EXCELLENCE

    There is only one way to achieve perfection; as whatever you do, you do it to your own satisfaction, we always make ourselves halt at mediocrity, maybe because of laziness or lack of interest (power of purpose), deadline (poor time management), greed etc., but this kind of attitude sabotage your whole future in that activity, either it is a fitness program, work, you need to correct your attitude for achieving excellence.

    You do the work----→ leak points came out--→mediocre work--→mediocre life.

    As your work reflects the environment within you, and with the reflection of your work either by outside feedback or internal satisfaction, due to which three main factors came up responsible or must be closely examine, they are:

1)   Attitude
2)   Purpose full life
3)   Self awareness and management.

To achieve excellence you need to make all these three

factors to be work on intellectually.

ATTITUDE

Attitude is the main factor for excellence and indirectly to the succeed in anything, which also shows the man worth, but only few are able to understand the importance of it, to explain the concept let's take an example of a sports person, in his 19, he was selected to play in an international cricket match against Pakistan but because of fast ball he got hit and his ear was bleeding, everyone suggested him to go back, it's his attitude which made him play that day and won the match, today he is called by the brand name Sachin Tendulkar, his attitude made him big otherwise he was as small as playing his first match.

OPEN-MINDED

Open minded makes you not struck in the defensive mind state but to acquire from even critics and make them work for you and make your work move towards perfection, open-mindedness in my terms is describe as the ability to welcome all the situations and focus on good things and search only opportunities in them and also enables you to absorb critics and use them in good way for example your friends says your new business idea is not worthy and being a close mind, you became angry at them and start working on it and also invest your savings in it due to which at the end you got nothing but lost your saving and time on the other hand you now acts as a open minded person and same situation happened but here instead of starting you modify the idea and start working with more feedback due to which end is much better than for close-minded one.

Mindset

You cannot achieve high ambitious aim with the same mindset

There is a mindset you need to acquire which is called entrepreneurial mindset, because an entrepreneur not only develop new technology, new product or service but also make its sales happened in major quantity, that's is why entrepreneurial journey makes you acquire great skills and makes you a better person, due to Information Age we have a vast knowledge of entrepreneurial mind set after analyses the life of great entrepreneurs.

With the proper mindset and its sustainability, you accidently develop some of the qualities like anti fragile (learn from hard failures and not let them break your spirit) or resilience (be optimistic in adverse situation), high confidence and personal style that is why, attaining mindset of entrepreneurship and lotus develops you personally and let you learn from real life examples rather than schools or books only; to cultivate entrepreneurial mindset, spirituality plays an essential role over development of your lotus mindset as either you learn and grow your mentality from hard experience and positive attitude or directly goes up with the help of spirituality.

It's better way to first develop your mindset and this mindset will enables you to learn and thrive as much as you can and ultimately makes you successful because due to this mindset you already visualize success and choose only success path sub consciously so attain your mindset first in order to succeed.

FILTERING CRITICISM

When negative critics appear for you or for your work, you no need to be panic because your short term thinking makes you in defensive position but if you think long term you will activate your learning system and can even take advantage from your enemies like your negative critics

As power of purpose came into play here the more desperate you are for your purpose the more likely you will able to learn from critics, Elon Musk always says that behind his success there is negative critics which he utilizes very wisely.

When negative critics appear ask questions like:

▪   Does the critic have any emotional problem of jealous or fear?

- Is there is any situation he or she faced which made him say that?
- What is the critic's background?
- Or is he or she is saying something better which will help my work improvise?
- Negative critics not only improvise your work but also give you a deep satisfaction level due to which you will more likely draw an excellent and creative work.

RITUALS AND HABITS
Wealthy habits:

Information age gives an enormous advantage of knowledge sharing, for example you love fashion but never think to make contribution in it, but in this age you will be able to read part time about fashion industry from all over the world and create your own designs, which you can test and improve your skills from feedback (I always believe that feedbacks are for improvement), the more your desperation in the industry the more will be the success rate in it, you can't blame others for your success status its always on you (your attitude, your beliefs) so if you feel that people are bad and world is hell to live in, it's just because you have created a wrong mindset which will not take you to your ambition level, as world will be the same as always it's on your mindset you have created which will give you desired success and happiness. Knowledge helps your idea become a clear imagination, so the easiest way to succeed or even take steps towards success is by cultivating wealthy habits(which you came across many times on facebook if you have subscribed to entrepreneurship pages) wealthy habits like reading nonfiction, invest in yourself, etc, as Bill Gates once said if I can have the super power I will prefer to have power of speed reading.

Nobody is rich, rich is the habits and rituals which make compound effects and slowly takes you on the journey of success, makes you able to acquire the wealth. You may have heard many cases where an individual gets rich either by lottery or some other means but eventually due to lack of financial intelligence, they soon lost it, if you acquire wealthy habits you will be able to acquire wealth.

Rituals helps you to develop your accurate habit and every person based on his strengths need to develop some more unique habits for their strength.

Aesthetics

By definition it is the branch of philosophy dealing with beauty and taste, when you start living your purpose in any field, it is better to have the aesthetic sense for your purpose due to which the great sense of marketing indirectly generated into you, Steve Jobs had the great sense of this science due to which he was able to generate huge revenue, because of his sense of aesthetics, he was able to disrupt the industry and the Apple products dominates the industry, so aesthetics with life purpose is a great merger which has the potential to takes you higher in career.

Personal development and innovation age:

From ages man has different tools which is required to rule over the world as from stone age he was needed mass amount of people to hunt or to acquire another village, then in middle age it is the tools and weapons which make a man ahead of the human race as for example Genghis khan and his kingdom had invented bow(made of composite objects) and arrow and which made him rule almost the whole world, In industrial age you are king if you have money which made you to have all the resources you need for rule and make your own kingdom, now in the current age you need to have problem solving attitude merge with knowledge and skills to be ahead of the world as 'solve billion people problem to be a billionaire' but now for the next age you need to find your purpose(even unclear) and then develop yourself and move forward with your purpose by the power of personal development which is next generation tool even its sound very old concept.

CHAPTER 7

Execution

"The master of the art of living makes little distinction between his work and his play, his labor and his leisure, his mind and his body, his education and his recreation, his love and his religion. He hardly knows which is which; he simply pursues his vision of excellence in whatever he does, leaving others to decide whether he is working or playing. To him he is always doing both."

Buddha

Success is directly proportional to the power of execution, Many people can't execute because throughout their life, they never realize their potential, they are in the rat race or part of somebody else's master plan, Everyone has their own motivation factor, Some are motivated by end results, some by their power, and some from their interests. Motivation helps them to keep going in life. Now, imagine if people use these motivational factors full-time for their career and get out from the system, first morally then intellectually and then physically. They can escape the system that was created by few people's dreams or plans. For example, Google is a great company of our time that is able to influence almost the entire world as not only able to contribute greatly to the world, but to also have created a master plan for others, as great engineers and budding entrepreneurs with great ideas came out from the college, hired by Google immediately or acquire their company (either friendly or hostile way) so that no other company can emerge in the economy, now think this master plan for ordinary society in which you got great academic scores and company hires you with great pay, in the beginning you will enjoy the great pay but as life goes on you will start bore because you are not contributing to the world and bore with the luxury(as mentioned earlier, luxury is for creativity and not a goal) and now imagine you came out of college with good grades with believe in yourself and start living your purpose then sooner or later you might be as big as the company hired you before, life is all about long term thinking because think you in 5 years or 10 years in aspect of your work or contribution, Now imagine you start living your purpose and in the last days of your life, you will see the great contributions you have made which will leave you, in a sense, to die as a king and not as a slave of money.

To get started there is a framework that consists of four domains of motivation in which you can put yourself and able to get started as soon you choose the path of life soon you will be able to achieve and contribute much and after aware all the four motivation go deep down and filter your thoughts with this framework and ask yourself which is greatest motivation factor for me again and again by which you will be able to intellectually achieve your goal or purpose of life by the help of awareness of deep motivation factor filtered by this framework (I suggest you to try meditation first) if this framework can't help you then take help from god by spirituality and you will be able to listen to your soul which will tells you the ultimate motivation factor because many of us are unclear because of surroundings influence and their big dreams imaginations because we falls between the cognition for ourselves and for others so you need to connect to your soul first if you can't figure out your callings.

Four focused areas are:
1) Problem focused
2) Interest focused
3) Strength focused
4) Reward focused

Problem focused Motivation

This motivation occurred with the negative emotions towards a problem which triggered you to solve it anyhow, for example Henry ford when he was a child he faced the problem of transportation but he was motivated enough to think crazy and imagine the concept of car and bold enough to execute his crazy imagination and literally changed the world with his imagination, even today automobile industry is growing rapidly, but the condition is you need to believe in yourself as much to solve the problem with your imagination as he said once the man who thinks he can't do or can do, in both of the cases he is right, so think again are you bold enough if not develop yourself with others intellect work presented via books and then be bold enough to live your dreams, problem can be from basic or personal to global level just solve and contribute to the world.

Interest focused Motivation

We all have interest in something, either it is basic sports to new generation technology such as artificial intelligence and machine learning but the fact that we are not bold enough to live it and neglect the idea by your own cognitive negative process which is influenced by others (that the idea is too big or small to make into a career) but you only live once and if you live it for the basic needs of human life make it more comfortable then you are only an ordinary person or even like animal (no contribution) but if you really want to live life with joy and satisfaction and also with financial security then you need to be crazy and bold enough to live your interest, however in the beginning you will face difficulties and even perceptually more because of your brain will create negative stories and show opposition to the idea, but consider it learning for your career, think of a child as if he stops walking because of fear to fall then he might end up with no legs, but even child is bold to get up again and again to become master or an athlete.

Strength focused motivation

Many people have the unique abilities, skills and strength and they love to use these unique abilities for others and for themselves, but over time and influence of others they don't use these skills much to the nil and completely neglect the god gift, but you need to become more aware, start small and even hire a consultant who can use his observation and update information, makes you aware of what big you can do with this unique abilities or what career is best for you which makes you use your abilities, many times we neglect our potential because of a competitive mind and see other as have sharp skill of same strength and rather than sharp your own ability you end up giving up your ability to use but if you love to use this ability you need to move with it and develop this ability and yourself to use it with excellence and make a career around it and again due to influence of this next age you also need to think differentiation to use this in the world.

Reward focused

Many people are motivated by the life and they just want to change their current living standard, because their philosophy is to earn and live lavishly, no other thought motivates them (mainly all of us are belongs to this category) for that the best way is to involve with the new emerging technology as AI, 3D printer etc. because of the influence of the innovation age, all the business cycles will have short cycle, and traditional business won't make you rich or the life you want and you need to ride on monopoly industries, start by any entrepreneur, intimate and create the business around his concept with observing all the weak points of it and create the venture by fixing that points, many people started with this motivation factor and end up discovering themselves in one of the above motivation factor(strength or interest focused) but the main part is this factor makes them able to act.

Resonate with the leader

When you can't find your motivation factor to start and struck within you own thoughts, then this technique might help, because of information age people get to know the leaders of all the field whetherit's sports or business and feel their career for themselves because their motivation factor is that feeling or that moment of feeling and because you even start making plan subconsciously to get that position and you act and on the way journey you develop yourself and get on the right path and succeed.

Living purpose made easy

This topic aims to give you a cognitive ease by providing some ways to get started and you will able to start working on your dream and can have more vivid imagination towards your purpose as apart from motivation techniques this topic is for cognitive ease and divided into four points as every point for motivation factor and also provided a mind mapping for that (as shown in figure and sorry for bad drawing and hand writing).

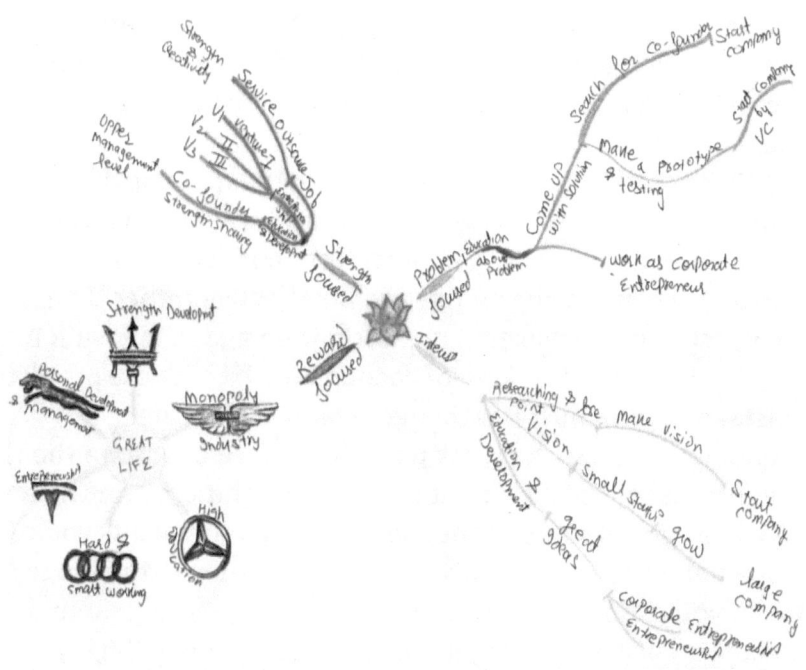

CHAPTER 8

Business model innovation

This chapters aims in to provide the basic idea of how creativity works in business model generation and also to shift your thinking paradigm of your less control over business model to have your own model type, thinking creatively for the business model generation, because in this highly capitalized world where innovation rate is going higher in which people are able to provide their creative solutions and uses their creativity to create their own business model.

This creative idea is generated with the merging of innovation age and entrepreneurship, unlike traditional business and systems which runs on well organized manner by high executives, due to which you need to be effective rather than efficient, but due to transition of information age to innovation age

Business model is kind of cocoon, in which idea is protected and instead cocoon bust it rather grow and absorb the surroundings, the less the weak points are there of cocoon the less will be the chances of it to burst or bankrupt, this chapter will not make you aware of some of the models and all the points you need to protect and have a innovative solution for them in the model but also help you choose your own business model which merge with your competency and style of management to work in highly optimum and efficient manner, there are also the models, which are decided on the basis of your product or services but if you want to choose your model you can go by this method and use your creativity even in running the business.

This chapter divides into four parts

Business model innovation on the basis of

1) Management style
2) Product and services
3) Future goals
4) Current trends

business model innovation which is based on the factors given below, are the key points need to consider before writing a business model or even to innovate it, for example you can out source manufacturing part of your business from your key partners and focus on the core values you are giving to the customers.

The 9 parts of any business model created by the authors of business model generation are:

1) Customers
2) Business value
3) Distribution
4) Relationship with customer
5) Revenue
6) Resources
7) Operations
8) Partners
9) Cost structure

Management style and business model innovation

you have a product or say an idea and due to knowledge of business model creation, you organize a model like your revenue stream or your distribution etc, and also created the strategic competency for your idea, but after execution you notice that as you grow with the business and your personal competencies are also increases and these competencies are now able to increase the competency of the business, this is inevitable for every venture, but now before hand if you are aware of your future competencies(core strengths and skills), rather than design the traditional model, but proactively design the model under consideration of your leadership, skills and development.

Let's say you have networking style of management and you are designing your business model for idea of big data technology (aims at suggestions in books), rather than design the business model on the basis of demand of product but you are designing in your own manner, it's the creativity that matters here and the more you use this muscle the more it will develop, because innovation age demands creativity. Now coming back to the model merging with your own style of management, you create the model whose all variables are protected by well organized system by either managing yourself or giving it to others to manage and Let the two variables under your control which are customer relationship and key partnership, because of your competency in networking you will be able to innovate, not only in terms of your product or service, but also in terms of business model, which gives exponential results to you, and the pace of which will be greater than others.

For every management style, an individual have to take charge for the callings of inner competencies, for example, for thinking management style it is value proposition and key resources and also cost structure and for achieving style it is the channels and revenue streams which need to be open for your creativity in the model, remember this is a hypothesis which gives you the basic idea of how you can use your creativity to the model also

In HCL India when new CEO Vinnet Nayyar was appointed, he did the turnaround the business model and shows creativity over key resource area by the program called employee first and customer second, which was criticized by many in the beginning and when it turn to be a great performer company employees or job seeker sees the company as best company to work on and a strategic sees it as best policy for an IT company (as key resources are employees and their welfare gave company great performance) and Vineet Nayaar sees it the only way to grow.

Models on the basis of your innovative product and service

Your creative product or service are sometimes need to run under a specific business model and which is design for the product in order to create enough influence to the customers, for example, you have an innovative product which solves a day to day activity of people, but you don't know how to increase revenue and promote the product, due to which your current situation needs to modify your model and turnaround it by focusing on building key partners(who has already created influence for the products like yours example QVC), due to which it makes your product a great pace which you couldn't do by yourself.

On the basis of future goals

Many times entrepreneurs struck in the middle and can't decide what they really want from the business, for that, ask yourself these questions and be clear and about the design of the business model, questions like is this model is for money ? Or for product development or creating value for customers etc., as business for money are kind of short term goal or less scope of development is there in your vision for the company and value creation is kind of long term goal in which you have a great vision in mind for the company.

By keeping your goals in mind you can generate your model beforehand so that your model strategy only execute for your goals only, just like coding for a program to execute particular activity. By having the knowledge of business model and how it works and form, you can code your business model too.

Business model created under consider of market demand or trends

For example now a day's trend is to promote via social media and make communication through that only, many times it is happened in the corporate world that you have to adopt the innovations and creativity of others, because it is better way to move forward, as this innovation age is all about switching to new, for example my creativity is best in product development and making a great product, where as yours is in commerce part, due to which we can create a great company(Apple inc.), many times you not able to create your way and for that you have to personally outsource the competency or simply intimate the innovation or even the business model and you stick to your core activity of entrepreneurship on the basis of your creation.

CHAPTER 9

New age business concepts

Steve jobs once said in his speech while motivating his employees that he wants to acquire the information age up to the most, as Apple, Microsoft or Google and even Facebook all are innovative companies which acquired most of the information age market but as they already embedded their roots in the information age, also creating the consequence which indirectly contributing and accelerating in transition to innovation age due to which by awareness proactive approach an entrepreneur need to develop the company which will capture the next age and its market, make the innovative companies which will be required in the next age, for example become a platform for the sharing of patents or any intellectual property by considering the view point of innovation age.

If you will make your career in Artificial intelligence, 3D printing, nano science, etc., your career will be secured, you need to think about your purpose, your strengths and ask yourself how can you contribute to the new age or even how can I develop myself to contribute in the innovation age.

Following are some technology examples

ARTIFICIAL INTELLIGENCE AND MACHINE LEARNING

Artificial Intelligence: interface between information age and innovation age

We all need a friend, a mentor and a lover who understands us well, who cares about us, who guide us, for that human have created a technology which is the artificial intelligence, and after more and more simplification and innovation will become a great friend to create and innovate with the colors of human emotions and field of interest, for example a basket ball coach has an creative idea to coach his students and after using artificial intelligence, he is not only able to overcome his weakness to create but also helps him for test results, make a prototype etc. There are many fields, it can be used, based on intelligence to use the technology, we will learn along the way as we move on with this technology, we can make it a friend of highly intellect friend who has super intelligence and super-informative as we can code our artificial friend with the characteristics of say Einstein or Holmes to guide us to help us out and work with as 10 thousand men capability following will be

A) **Manufacturing with your own:** Artificial intelligence when merge with the 3D printing technology can create highly effective prototypes in cost effective way, for example you have this great idea which excites you too much is of 'gadget organizer', which you think will be highly demanding but you also think it will cost you too much as all of your savings, due to which your fear will be more than excitement but with these combination this saturation of information age and innovation age will come soon, as cost of 3D printing is going down due to which soon AI and 3D will give a great boom to innovation age.

B) **God like working:** In our life time, we came across with several days or even months when we feel great, think great, and have god speed in our work due to our mindset, motivation level, soothe emotions etc, but we can't sustain this pleasure for more and become again part of mediocrity and low pleasure living, but after having super artificial friend, we will be able to record that situation enables us to have god power for example recording of emotions level (reading of levels of four basic emotions governed humans) or asking help from AI, as what are the mind set needs required to achieve the challenge, for example real life story is one of my uncle who is a doctor age: 53 had a space for the kids school and was thinking to give it on lease, he went to the franchisee of a school owner and after discussion there was a point where the school owner asked him to manage the school them self, but because it needs to be a certain different kind of mindset than the one required to be a businessman, he refused and the owner taunt him that you will always be a service class, this situation shows different activities need different mindset, so after this great mind blower AI friend you will be able to get the mindset based on work you want to achieve.

C) **Be your own doctor:** There are certain types, indications, biochemical readings etc, which can predict the status of the health of the individual; for example you experience laziness and you think your work load makes you feel that, but your body knows well, as lack of vitamin D can be factor, Health upmost level can be achieved by nanotechnology merge with medical science and artificial intelligence will not only makes you healthy (nanocrystal designed to sense whole body sync with the artificial intelligence which is equipped by medical science gives you on the way doctor).

D) **Make world heaven on earth:** By artificial intelligence we not only predict the natural disaster, but also can change the human mental state from a criminal mindset to ideal human state.

As possibilities and limitations are in mind not in technology

Big Data

Increase in population and increased data from them, due to which this technology of Big Data helps us to organize the data and use it in analysis the trends and also influence customers. For marketers this technology will be disruptive in future, due to which with marketing sense and big data and a sense of analytics, in order to have a creative edge in innovation age, also big data can be used in many business to business or business to customer areas in which with the help of data you can predict future predictions and due to which it will help in product development by calculating the customer preferences.

Innovative ideas:

1)   Filtration: In which you can search your desired product or service around the world, for example your customer have a taste to read a unique topic and by big data you can filter the search and show the customer only desired search options which will help him to make better decision and save a lot of time.

2)   Research: The Company which help other business to show the trend and future scope for their product and service.

3)   Can help in decision making in government level too.

3D Printing

Imagine 3 D printers at the time of Leonardo da Vinci, when he can have all the prototypes of his creative ideas, which were on papers only and after making prototype, the king might invest in his crazy for that time ideas and change the world, 3D printers can be disruptive in manufacturing because of continuously dropping of cost per print, due to which in future manufacturing will be very easy to operate, even 3D printer merge with AI can create product for you and you won't need to buy anything from market.

Human potential

Advancement in medical industry as well as all the other technologies will allow us to creatively merge them and creates new systems for ourselves in terms of our potential, efficiency and effectiveness as the more we know about any technology the more efficiency we can have from the machine and human itself a emotional machine, in future we can hack our neuron-chemicals which will allow us to increase our productivity and creativity, by merging artificial intelligence with bio medical sensors with neuron-chemical science will rise the concept of hacking the neuron-chemicals our body and will make us into super humans category.

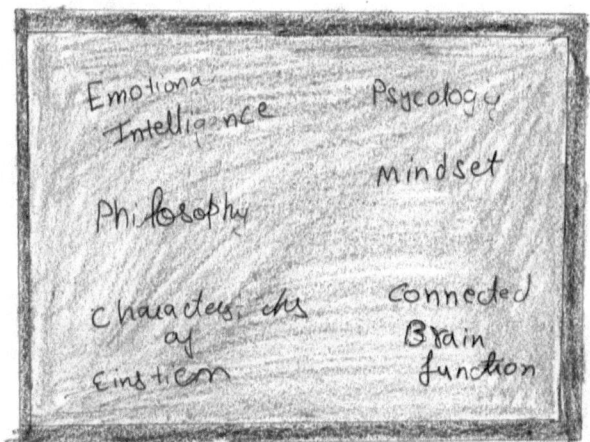

Emotional
Intelligence

Psycology

Mindset

Philosophy

Characteristics
of
Einstien

Connected
Brain
function

Machine learning

CHAPTER 10

Sample Business Idea to Contribute from College itself

EUREKA FOR EVERYONE

This company's main role is to develop products and services to help the innovators to invent for example an app or an article to make the laggards to move toward innovators (as there is a cycle in human generation from innovators to early adopters to laggards), vision is to make a group of people (kind of master mind group) who works in accordance of the innovation age, just like after internet was invented, Facebook shaped the information age likewise when we know innovation age is coming we need to build companies to cater it and become the great contributor for shaping the next age.

In the beginning, company will develop invention design, creative applications, and business strategies for existing companies and improvising, marketing plans; anything creative is a product of it, and later on as per the conditions will emerge with the innovation age, company will follow the trend.

Sample Business Model
Customer Segments:
Large companies, mass market, small company's owners, Entrepreneurs.
Value Proposition:
Efficiency
Channels:
Personal assistance, self service
Revenue Streams:
Licensing, Asset sales
Key Resources:
Intellectual
Key Activities:
Problem solving
Key Partnership:
Legal firms, Consultants
Cost Structure:
Testing and registration

EPILOGUE

I hope you enjoyed the book at least some parts of it, and many of you will think some of the theories of the book mere hypothetic but many of them are useful for you if you give them a try, my main aim was to make you proactive about future because it will be survival of the fittest scene, as of increase in population and rise in competition and the only way out is follow the trend of innovation which will be empower by the power of your life purpose and innovation or differentiation,

I apologize for my drawings and not effective writing, I wrote this book for the people and not for the pleasure due to which I neglect the variable of pleasure in writing but you will find this book interesting because it is based on creativity, innovation, entrepreneurship and spirituality.

AKSHAY BANSAL

Akshaybansal89@gmail.com

www.ingramcontent.com/pod-product-compliance
Lightning Source LLC
Chambersburg PA
CBHW021411170526
45164CB00002B/603